Will You Transition?

JONATHAN JACKSON, LMFTA, MBA

Published by

KARIMA Publishing

An imprint of KARIMA Solutions, PLLC

Published by KARIMA Publishing, an imprint of KARIMA Solutions, PLLC

This book is intended for educational, inspirational, and reflective purposes only. It is not a substitute for psychotherapy, medical care, crisis intervention, legal advice, or other professional services. If you are experiencing significant emotional distress or are in crisis, please seek support from a licensed professional or emergency services in your area.

Published in the United States of America

KARIMA Publishing
An imprint of KARIMA Solutions, PLLC
PO Box 6932
Tacoma, WA 98417
www.karimasolutions.com

First Edition
ISBN: 979-8-950894-00-8

Book design by: Jonathan Jackson, LMFTA, MBA

Healing should not be a luxury.
And yet for far too many individuals, couples, and families, access to quality mental health care remains financially out of reach.
That reality matters deeply to me.

As a therapist, I have seen firsthand what happens when people are ready for healing but cannot access support. I believe that access to transformative care should not be reserved only for those with financial privilege.

That is why

50% OF NET PROFITS FROM EVERY SALE OF

Will You Transition?

ARE DIRECTED TO THE KARIMA THERAPY ACCESS FUND.

The KARIMA Therapy Access Fund exists to help subsidize therapy services for individuals, couples, and families who would otherwise be unable to afford care.
Because healing multiplies. Stories matter.
And transformed lives create transformed communities.

WANT TO HELP EXPAND ACCESS EVEN FURTHER?
Scan the QR code below to make a direct contribution.

or visit:
www.karimasolutions.com/donate

THANK YOU FOR HELPING MAKE HEALING MORE ACCESSIBLE!

ABOUT THE AUTHOR

Jonathan Jackson is a therapist, strategist, educator, speaker, and spoken word storyteller whose work sits at the intersection of healing, leadership, identity, and transformation.

As the founder of KARIMA Solutions, PLLC, Jonathan helps individuals, couples, organizations, schools, and communities reauthor their stories and shape what's next.

His work blends therapeutic insight, strategic thinking, and the transformative power of storytelling to create experiences that move people. Not just emotionally, but practically.

Jonathan is an experienced speaker, known for engaging keynote presentations, plenary talks, workshops, leadership development experiences, curriculum design, facilitation, and spoken word performances that challenge audiences to think differently, feel deeply, and move intentionally. Whether speaking to educators, nonprofit leaders, corporate teams, faith communities, or audiences seeking personal transformation, Jonathan brings a rare blend of clinical depth, emotional intelligence, executive strategy, lived authenticity, and unforgettable storytelling.

His spoken word performances have moved audiences across the pacific northwest, while his professional work spans therapy, consulting, education, leadership development, and systems transformation.

At the heart of Jonathan's work is a simple belief:
The stories we live by shape the lives we lead...

CONNECT WITH JONATHAN
Instagram & YouTube: @mrjonathanjackson | @karimasolutions
Website: karimasolutions.com | LinkedIn: linkedin.com/in/jjackson253

BRING JONATHAN TO YOUR ORGANIZATION
Jonathan is available for:

- keynote presentations
- conference plenaries
- workshops & retreats
- spoken word performances

Scan to connect, or email: info@karimasolutions.com

THIS BOOK IS NOT THERAPY

It is not intended to diagnose, treat, cure, or prevent any mental health condition. *The poems, reflections, questions, and exercises contained within these pages are educational and informational in nature* and should not be considered a substitute for professional mental health care, psychological treatment, medical advice, crisis intervention, or ongoing therapy.

While self-reflection can be powerful, there are times when healing is best pursued with the support of a trained professional. If you are experiencing persistent sadness, anxiety, trauma-related symptoms, relationship distress, thoughts of self-harm, substance use concerns, overwhelming stress, or other mental health challenges, I encourage you to seek support from a qualified mental health professional in your area. You do not have to navigate difficult seasons alone.

As a Licensed Marriage and Family Therapist Associate (LMFTA) in the State of Washington, I have the privilege of walking alongside individuals, partners, and families as they navigate life's challenges and transitions. If you are interested in exploring whether we might be a good fit for a therapeutic relationship, I invite you to visit www.karimasolutions.com to learn more about my practice and available services.

IF YOU ARE IN CRISIS

If you believe you may be experiencing a mental health emergency, are considering harming yourself, or are concerned about the immediate safety of yourself or another person, please seek emergency assistance immediately. *If you are in the United States and Canada:*

988 Suicide & Crisis Lifeline
Call or text 988
Available 24 hours a day, 7 days a week.

If you are outside the United States, contact your local emergency services, crisis hotline, healthcare provider, or mental health support organization for immediate assistance. Help is available. You matter. And whatever chapter you are currently living through, there are people ready and willing to help you carry it.

DEDICATION

For those who kept going
when stillness felt unbearable.

For those who learned to survive
before they ever learned to breathe.

For those who outgrew identities
they once needed to stay alive.

For those standing at the threshold
between understanding and action.

And for anyone finally ready
to stop asking whether change is possible
and answer the question:

Will You Transition?

Transformation is often spoken about as though it happens in solitude. As though growth is some quiet, isolated act of will. But the truth is, even the most personal journeys are often shaped by the presence, encouragement, and grace of others who help steady us along the way. This book may have been written through my hands, but it was not created in isolation.

Shar,
Thank you for being my rock, my partner, and one of the clearest manifestations of grace in this season of my life. Your presence has been nothing short of a blessing. You have brought peace where there was once noise, steadiness where there was uncertainty, and a kind of partnership that has challenged me to grow. Not through pressure, but through presence. Thank you for loving me in ways that feel grounding rather than demanding. For helping me breathe more deeply. For helping me trust more fully. For walking with me through this season of transformation. And perhaps most meaningfully, thank you for the role you have played in deepening my spiritual journey. For the conversations, the prayers, the reflections, and the quiet reminders that faith is not merely something we profess. It is something we practice.
I am profoundly grateful that our paths crossed when they did.

CONTENTS

A NOTE BEFORE YOU BEGIN

Before you turn these pages, pause...
This is not meant to be something you rush through. It's not meant to be consumed in a single sitting or checked off like a task completed. This is a space you enter. A journey you walk. Not just a window into my story. A mirror you hold up to your own.

Every piece in this collection was written from a place of real vulnerability. Not polished. Not performative. These poems trace my own long and often difficult road into relationship with God. A road marked by questions, resistance, growth, surrender. A road where I thought I was searching for Him, only to realize He had been walking beside me all along. In moments I misunderstood. In seasons I tried to outrun. In spaces where I felt alone. He was present, patient, and preparing me.

This is not a story of perfection. It is a story of becoming. And because of that, this book is not meant to be read passively.

It is meant to be experienced.

This collection is intentionally designed as more than a reading experience. It is an invitation into reflection, integration, and movement.

You will encounter:

BRIDGES
Brief reflections that introduce the emotional terrain ahead, helping frame the poem not simply as art, but as invitation.

POEMS
The heartbeat of the work. Some may feel familiar. Some may challenge you. Some may say aloud what you have only ever whispered internally.

NOTICING & INTEGRATION
A space to slow down and pay attention to what surfaced for you. Through reflective questions and scaling prompts, you are invited to notice your patterns, your stories, your assumptions, and your opportunities for growth.

WHAT'S ALREADY TRUE
A space to notice what may already be working, shifting, or quietly becoming true in your life. These questions invite you to look for evidence of strength, movement, and possibility that may have gone unnoticed.

MICRO PRACTICE
Transformation does not happen through insight alone. Each exercise is designed to help you move what you've noticed from thought into action. From reflection into embodiment.

CARRY THIS FORWARD
A final invitation to leave each section with something more than understanding. A truth to hold. A question to revisit. A decision to practice.

There is no "right" pace for this work. Some readers may move through a section each day. Others may spend an entire week with a single poem. Both are valid.

The goal is not to finish this book. The goal is to let it move you.

So, underline what resonates. Journal honestly. Pause when something feels uncomfortable. Return when you need to. And most importantly, be gentle with yourself.

Transformation is rarely linear. But if you remain open, honest, and willing...it is absolutely possible.

The goal of this collection is not just understanding... Not just alignment...

THE GOAL OF THIS COLLECTION IS TRANSITION.

SEARCHING

I went looking for God...
In stained glass windows and pulpits wrapped in gold.
In choirs lifting voices high enough to scrape the ceiling of heaven.
I searched the pages of holy books.
Hands trembling like they might open a portal if I read the words just right.
But the voice I longed for wasn't in the thunder.
It was in the whisper.
It wasn't up there, It was right here.
See, I had been praying all along.
But I didn't know that the Amen I was chasing was the echo of my own spirit.
That every silent plea I spoke to the sky was answered by the stillness rising in my chest.

I thought divinity was somewhere outside of me.
A flame I had to earn.
A secret hidden on a mountaintop.
But I found it in the mirror.
In the tears that slipped uninvited down my cheeks.
In the quiet realization that I have always been accompanied.
In the undefeated part of me that refused to bow to the storm.
When I found myself, I found Him.
And I realized the only way I could find myself was through Him.

I discovered that God is not a voice booming from the clouds, but the compass you carry when the map has burned.
God is the breath you catch when you thought you couldn't.
God is the way your scars sing lullabies of survival.
I found coverage in my curiosity.
Sanctuary in my searching.
Prophecy in my persistence.
And when I finally fell to my knees, it wasn't in defeat.
It was in recognition.
That in finding myself...My true self.
The me beneath the masks of survival.
What I had actually found was God...
For there is no me without Him.

NOTICING & INTEGRATION

THE SEARCH

Sometimes we spend years looking for something without realizing what we are actually searching for.

- What have you spent significant time searching for outside of yourself?
- What did you hope finding it would give you?
- What have you discovered about yourself through the search itself?
- On a scale of 1–10, how connected do you currently feel to your deepest values, beliefs, or sense of purpose?
- What would be different if that number were one point higher?

BENEATH THE MASKS

This poem suggests that there is a version of us beneath survival, performance, and expectation.

- What roles, masks, or identities have you learned to wear in order to navigate life?
- When do you feel most connected to the version of yourself that exists beneath those roles?
- What helps that version of you emerge more fully?
- On a scale of 1–10, how comfortable do you feel showing up as your authentic self?
- What would tell you that you had moved one point closer to the version of yourself you want to be more consistently?

MEANING & RECOGNITION

Sometimes growth is less about discovering something new and more about recognizing what has been present all along.

- Looking back, what experiences now seem more meaningful than they did at the time?
- What strengths have carried you through difficult seasons, even when you did not fully acknowledge them?
- What part of your story are you beginning to see differently?
- How clearly can you recognize the strengths, lessons, and growth that have emerged from your life experiences?
- If you were one point higher, what part of your story would you stop minimizing, dismissing, or overlooking?

WHAT'S ALREADY TRUE

Sometimes growth is not about discovering something new. Sometimes it is about recognizing what has been present all along. The strength you needed may have already been carrying you. The guidance you were seeking may have been quietly unfolding. The truth you're searching for may be something you've known for far longer than you realize.

- Where in your life do you already see evidence that you have been guided, supported, or sustained through difficult seasons?
- What part of yourself has remained present and resilient, even when circumstances tried to convince you otherwise?
- What strengths, values, or truths have been quietly accompanying you long before you learned to name them?

MICRO PRACTICE

THE RECOGNITION INVENTORY

Sometimes transformation begins not with finding something new, but with recognizing what is already there.

Complete the following statements:

WHAT HAS CARRIED ME

Looking back, I can now see that ____ helped carry me through difficult seasons.

WHAT REMAINS

No matter what I have experienced, ____ has remained true about me.

WHAT I AM LEARNING

I am beginning to understand that ____.

WHAT I TRUST

The part of me that continues to move forward, even when things are difficult, is ____.

WHAT I WILL HONOR

Moving forward, I want to make more room in my life for ____.

CARRY THIS FORWARD

Many people spend their lives searching. Searching for purpose. Searching for belonging. Searching for certainty. Searching for God. And sometimes the search is necessary. Sometimes we must wander long enough to recognize what has been walking beside us all along.

The goal is not to have every answer. The goal is to remain open enough to recognize truth when it arrives. To notice the strength that survived. To honor the wisdom that emerged. To trust the part of you that has continued to move forward, even when you could not see the path clearly.

Because sometimes what we call finding is really remembering. And sometimes what we discover is that we were never as alone as we thought.

SACRED SPACE

There is a strange irony in searching for something your whole life only to discover it was never absent.

Many of us spend years looking outward for direction, certainty, validation, or purpose. We search for answers in achievements, relationships, institutions, expectations, and opinions. We search for something that will finally tell us who we are.

But eventually a different question emerges. What if the thing we're looking for isn't somewhere else? What if the deepest truths about who we are have been waiting patiently beneath the noise all along?

Finding yourself is rarely a dramatic event. More often, it is a return. A return to the voice beneath the expectations. A return to the identity beneath the performance. A return to the self that existed before survival became a full-time occupation.

The challenge is that many of us have spent so long adapting to the world around us that we no longer recognize the sound of our own voice. We know how to be productive. We know how to be useful. We know how to be impressive. But we struggle to answer a much simpler question: Who am I when there is nothing to prove?

Before we can move forward, we must first create space to listen. The next piece is an invitation into that space. A place beneath the noise. Beneath the performance. Beneath the armor. A place where your truest self has been waiting patiently to be remembered.

SACRED SPACE

Before the words, there was the whisper.
Before the whisper, the wound.
Before the wound, the flesh that God built.
And then hid a piece of Himself inside.
And He said, "This part is mine."
The part that storms can't spoil.
That scarcity can't scar. That survival can't steal.

I thought I'd lost my voice.
Drowned it in the deadlines.
Buried it under duty.
Muted it beneath the manners I mistook for manhood.
But God said, "Son, I wasn't punishing you, I was preserving you."
Because if that didn't happen.
If I stayed in touch with or rediscovered that voice too soon.
I would've weaponized the very thing that was meant to heal me.
To heal others.

He tucked it in a sacred space.
Not to keep it from me, but to keep it for me.
And when I finally quieted the chaos long enough to listen, I heard it humming like a tune that was once stuck in my head but that I'd long since forgotten.
He hid it where the hurt couldn't reach.
Not to take it from me, but to protect it from the version of me that didn't yet know how to carry it.
Somewhere behind ribs that learned rhythm before they ever learned language.
Before I had the words to name what I was feeling.
Before I had the discipline to hold what I was asking for.
He placed it there.
And while I was out here building walls.
Trying to protect myself from everything that had ever broken me.
He was building something inside of me that didn't need protection.
It needed preparation.

I thought the silence was punishment.
I thought the distance meant denial.

I thought something had gone wrong.
But nothing was wrong.
I was being rehearsed.
Rehearsed for peace, not for applause.
Because applause requires performance.
But peace?
Peace requires alignment, and alignment has a pace.
A rhythm you don't set, you learn to follow.
While I was grinding, trying to force something into existence.
He was refining.
Removing what didn't belong.
Strengthening what did.
Waiting until I could receive what I kept trying to rush.

I used to beg for release.
From the pressure. From the stillness.
From the feeling of being held in a place that didn't make sense.
Now I thank Him for it.
For the restraint.
For the delay.
For the discipline disguised as distance.
Because what I thought was a cage was actually a covering.
And what I thought I was losing was the version of me that would have misused the very thing I was praying for.
I had to lose the mic to understand what I was supposed to say.
Had to stop performing to remember who I was without an audience.
Had to sit in the quiet long enough to realize I was never without a voice.
I was being taught how to use it.

There's a part of you untouched.
A holy remnant that never got the memo that you were broken.
The part that remembers Eden.
That hums hymns in the dark.
That keeps your name written in God's handwriting, even when the world tries to spell you small.
You didn't lose it.
You just needed to outgrow the noise that used to drown it.
You thought it was gone, but it was guarded.
You thought it was buried, but it was banked.

Interest compounding in your absence, waiting for your return.
You are exactly where you need to be.
Not a step early, not a syllable late.

My sound found me when I stopped searching for perfection and started listening for sense.
Now every poem is prayer.
Every audience is altar.
Every breath a baptism in purpose.
I was never mute, just marinating.
I was never voiceless, just being tuned.
The rest before the reprise.

There is a place inside you that trauma can't trespass.
That fear can't foreclose.
That shame can't sell.
That's your sacred space.
And when you find it.
When it is revealed to you.
Rest there.
Live there.
And when you finally open your mouth...
Let it sound like surrender.

NOTICING & INTEGRATION

IDENTITY & VOICE

Sometimes growth is less about becoming someone new and more about remembering who we were before fear, expectations, and survival strategies taught us to hide.

- When in your life have you felt most connected to your voice?
- What did that version of you believe about themselves that you may have forgotten?
- If your "sacred space" could speak, what would it say about who you really are?
- On a scale of 1–10, how connected do you currently feel to your authentic self?
- What is helping keep that number from being lower?

SILENCE & STORY

Many of us spend years interpreting silence as absence. But sometimes silence is not abandonment. Sometimes it is protection. Sometimes it is preparation. Sometimes it is an invitation to listen more deeply.

- What meanings have you attached to seasons of silence in your life?
- Where might you have interpreted protection as punishment?
- What might your silence have preserved that noise would have corrupted?
- On a scale of 1–10, how much trust do you currently have in seasons of uncertainty, waiting, or stillness?
- If you were one point higher on that scale, how would you show up differently in those seasons?

PERFORMANCE & PRESENCE

It is exhausting to spend your life auditioning for belonging. At some point, healing invites us to stop performing and start inhabiting our lives more fully. Not as who we think we should be. As who we actually are.

- In what areas of your life are you still performing instead of being?
- What would it look like to show up without needing to prove anything?
- Who are you when no one is watching, and how close is that to the version of you that others experience?
- On a scale of 1–10, how free do you feel to show up authentically in your daily life?
- What would be different about how you engage with other?

WHAT'S ALREADY TRUE

You do not have to create your truest self. You only have to become reacquainted with them. Sometimes what feels lost has simply been waiting for your attention.

- When recently, even briefly, did you feel aligned with your true self? What helped create that moment, and what might help you experience more moments like it?
- What evidence already exists that the part of you that you thought was gone is still very much alive?
- Where in your life do you already experience moments of peace, belonging, or authenticity, and what do those moments reveal about what your soul needs most?

MICRO PRACTICE

THE RETURN

Many of us spend years searching for something we believe is missing. A sense of peace. A sense of belonging. A sense of clarity. A sense of self. But what if the goal is not to find something new? What if the goal is to return to something that has been there all along?

Set aside 10–15 minutes.

Find a quiet space. Silence your phone. Take several slow breaths.

REMEMBER

Think of a time in your life when you felt deeply connected to yourself.

Not necessarily successful. Not necessarily happy. Simply connected. Write about that version of yourself. What did they value? What mattered to them? How did they move through the world?

RECOGNIZE

Complete the following:

The part of me that I miss most is ____.

I know this part of me is still present because ____.

One place I still see evidence of this part of myself is ____.

RECLAIM

What is one small action you could take this week that would help you reconnect with your truest self?

Write it down.
Make it specific.
Make it achievable.
Then commit to doing it within the next seven days.

RETURN

Complete this sentence:

As for me, I am someone who ____.

Write your answer slowly.
Write who you know yourself to be, not who you think you should be.
Read it aloud, then read it again.

CARRY THIS FORWARD

The world spends a great deal of time trying to tell us who we are.

Sometimes it does so directly. Sometimes through expectations. Sometimes through criticism. Sometimes through applause. But none of those things are the same as truth.

Truth lives deeper. Beneath performance. Beneath achievement. Beneath fear. Beneath every version of yourself you created in order to survive.

There is a part of you that has remained remarkably consistent through every season of your life. A part of you that existed before the disappointment. Before the heartbreak. Before the expectations. Before the pressure to become someone other than yourself.

That part is not lost. It does not need to be created. It only needs to be remembered. So, when life becomes noisy, return. When doubt becomes loud, return. When you find yourself performing, striving, or forgetting, return. Return to your values. Return to your truth. Return to the voice that knows who you are beneath every role you play.

Because the journey was never about becoming someone else. It was always about becoming more fully yourself. And that version of you has been waiting patiently the entire time.

Welcome home.

EXHALE

The hardest part about coming home to yourself is not finding the way. It's believing you're safe enough to stay.

For many of us, survival became second nature long before we realized it. We learned to stay alert. Stay productive. Stay prepared. Stay useful. We learned to anticipate disappointment before it arrived and solve problems before they became visible. At first, those strategies protected us. Then they became us.

We became so accustomed to carrying weight that we forgot what it felt like to set it down. So accustomed to tension that relaxation began to feel unfamiliar. So accustomed to earning our worth that simply existing felt irresponsible.

The body keeps score of these things. It remembers the seasons when you had to stay ready. The moments when rest felt unsafe. The years when slowing down felt like falling behind. And even when the danger has passed, the body often continues preparing for battles that are no longer taking place.

That is why self-discovery is not merely an intellectual exercise. It is physical. It is emotional. It is spiritual. Because before you can hear your own voice clearly, you may first need to release the noise your nervous system has been carrying for years. You may need to remember that not every moment requires vigilance. Not every season requires survival strategies. Not every breath needs to be held.

The next piece is an invitation to do something many of us have forgotten how to do. To stop gripping. To stop guarding. To stop bracing. And simply...breathe.

EXHALE

I didn't know how loud silence could be until I finally heard myself breathe.
Didn't know how heavy home could feel until I stepped outside the house and felt my chest return to me.
Didn't know how much I'd shrunk until the space around me widened and my ribs expanded like God was reminding them what fullness felt like.
There's a moment.
After the storm but before the sunlight.
Where your body remembers oxygen before your mind grants permission to breath.
A moment where you don't even trust the inhale because you've lived so long on borrowed breath that receiving abundance feels dangerous.
But then it hits.
Not the kind of breath you ration.
The kind that rips through you. Rushes in like revelation.
Fills every hollow you didn't know existed and whispers, "You're safe now."

When you leave a life that suffocates...
You don't just breathe.
The breath feels like a blessing.
Air becomes acceleration, your lungs become launchpads.
Every inhale is a resurrection, every exhale is a release.
And somehow...
Every step forward becomes two.
Every sunrise hits different.
Every mirror tells the truth.
I'm not just growing, I'm becoming.
Rapidly. Ruthlessly. Honestly.
In harmony with a God who's been waiting for me to breathe again.

What they don't tell you is that healing isn't quiet.
It's loud.
It's the sound of your nervous system rebooting.
It's the crackle of dead branches falling off your spirit.
It's the hum of peace returning like electricity after an outage.
I didn't realize how long I'd been bracing.
How long I'd been holding in.
Holding on.
Holding back.

How long I'd been starving my soul to feed my fear.
When you live in survival mode the inhale is shallow.
The exhale feels like risk.
You can't grow where you can't breathe.
I was dying politely.
Smiling while suffocating.

But when you return to yourself?
Every inhale feels like alignment.
Every exhale a release.
Every breath is a reminder that God didn't just save me.
He restored me.
Repaired me.
Rebuilt me.
Reinflated my lungs with his grace.

NOTICING & INTEGRATION

SURVIVAL AWARENESS

The body is remarkably adaptive. When life becomes difficult, uncertain, or painful, it learns to protect us. But sometimes the strategies that help us survive a difficult season continue long after the danger has passed.

- In what ways have you been operating in survival mode recently?
- What does survival look like for you (e.g., overworking, avoiding, controlling, staying busy, shutting down)?
- How do you know when your body is bracing for something that has yet to happen?
- On a scale of 1–10 (*10 being all the time*), how often do you feel like you are moving through life from a place of tension, vigilance, or self-protection?
- What would you do differently if you were one point lower?

BREATH & SAFETY

Many people spend years learning how to push through. Many of us never learn how to feel safe enough to soften. Exhale invites us to consider what helps us move from protection into presence.

- When was the last time you felt truly at ease in your body?
- What people, places, or experiences help you feel grounded and safe?
- What currently makes it hard to relax, trust, or let your guard down?
- On a scale of 1–10, how safe do you currently feel in your own body?
- What would be different if you were one point higher?

LETTING GO

We often carry things for far too long. Expectations. Responsibilities. Old stories. Sometimes healing begins when we stop asking how much more we can hold and start asking what we can release.

- What are you still carrying that your mind, body, or spirit may be ready to set down?
- What would it mean to trust that you do not have to carry everything anymore?
- What feels unfamiliar, but healthy, in your life right now?
- On a scale of 1–10, how comfortable are you allowing yourself to rest without guilt?
- If that number moved one point higher, what would you stop doing, stop carrying, or stop expecting of yourself?

WHAT'S ALREADY TRUE

Your nervous system already knows something about peace. Your body has already experienced moments of safety. Your life already contains evidence that survival is not the only way you know how to live.

- When was a recent moment, even briefly, where you felt calm, grounded, or at peace? What made that moment possible, and how might you create more of it?
- What are you already doing that the version of you in survival mode never would have allowed?
- Who are you when you are not operating from urgency, fear, or self-protection?

MICRO PRACTICE
THE PERMISSION TO EXHALE

Many of us know how to work. Many of us know how to endure. Many of us know how to keep going. The harder skill is learning how to stop. This exercise is not about forcing relaxation. It is about practicing permission.

Find a comfortable place to sit. Place both feet on the floor.
Set a timer for five minutes.

Complete five cycles of the following:

INHALE

Slowly through your nose for four seconds. As you inhale, silently say:

"I am here."

Hold for two seconds.

Allow yourself to simply notice.
No fixing.
No solving.
No performing.

EXHALE

Slowly through your mouth for six to eight seconds.

As you exhale, silently say:
"I don't need to carry this right now."

Repeat five times.

When you finish, place a hand on your chest and answer the following:

What feels lighter than it did five minutes ago?
What am I still carrying that may not belong to me?
What would it look like to offer myself the same compassion I so freely offer others?

Write whatever emerges.

No editing.
No judgment.
Just notice.

CARRY THIS FORWARD

You survived. Honor that. There were seasons when survival was wisdom. Seasons when vigilance protected you. Seasons when carrying everything felt necessary. But survival was never meant to become your permanent address. The skills that helped you endure are not the same skills that will help you flourish.

At some point, healing asks a different question. Not: "*How much more can I carry?"* But: *"What can I finally put down?"*

You were not created to spend your entire life bracing for impact. You were not created to hold your breath indefinitely. You were not created to mistake exhaustion for strength. Strength is not always found in endurance. Sometimes strength looks like trust. Sometimes strength looks like softness. Sometimes strength looks like allowing yourself to rest before you have "earned it."

So, this is your invitation. Not to push harder. Not to become more productive. Not to prove your worth through effort. But to practice something that may feel surprisingly unfamiliar. To pause. To soften. To trust. To breathe. To exhale.

Because peace is not something you must earn. Sometimes it is something you must allow. And perhaps the next chapter of your life begins not with striving. But with one long, honest breath.

HEAL THYSELF

Sometimes the first thing we notice after the noise quiets down is the voice that remained.

Not the voice of a parent. Not the voice of a teacher, partner, boss, or critic. Our own. The running commentary beneath every decision. The narrator behind every setback. The voice that explains who we are, what we're capable of, and what we deserve. Many of us spend years believing that our thoughts are simply facts. That the stories we tell ourselves are objective truth. That the labels we've carried are accurate descriptions rather than inherited interpretations.

But once we begin slowing down, something remarkable happens. We start hearing the language we've been living inside. The ways we diminish ourselves. The ways we disqualify ourselves. The ways we speak to ourselves with a level of harshness we would never direct toward someone we love. And perhaps that is one of the most overlooked realities of healing.

You cannot consistently build a life stronger than the story you believe about yourself. Because every action grows from identity. Every decision grows from belief. Every future grows from the language used to describe what is possible. If survival taught us to brace, it often also taught us to narrate ourselves through fear. Through limitation. Through old wounds that still believe they are protecting us.

Healing requires something different. Not pretending the pain never happened. Not ignoring the struggle. But becoming intentional about the story that gets to shape what happens next. Because eventually, the question is no longer: *"What happened to me?"* The question becomes: *"What am I saying to myself now?"*

The next piece is an invitation to reclaim that conversation. To become more intentional with the language that shapes your life. To recognize that every story can be rewritten. Including the one you're telling yourself.

HEAL THYSELF

There comes a moment.
Quiet, almost unremarkable.
When you finally realize you've been waiting for someone else to say something you were always meant to hear from yourself.
A moment when the echo of old criticism feels heavier than the truth you know.
When you catch yourself reaching outward for a gentleness you have never learned to practice inwardly.

That's the moment healing begins.
Not when the world apologizes.
Not when the past untangles itself.
But when you stand in front of your own reflection and decide to speak life where silence used to live.

Because the stories you tell yourself are not background noise.
They are blueprints.
Every thought is architecture.
Every word is scaffolding.
Every affirmation is a hammer building the life your spirit has been sketching for years.
The lies you inherited.
The ones wrapped in shame.
The ones spoken by people who were hurting themselves.
Those are just old drafts.
You don't owe your future to the language of your wounds.

Heal thyself doesn't mean pretend the pain never happened.
It means stop letting the pain narrate the version of you who's standing here now.
Because the brain believes what it hears often.
The heart believes what it feel gently.
The body believes what it senses consistently.

Imagine what would happen if softness became your mother tongue.
If strength became your second skin.
If "I can" became your morning ritual and "I'm enough" became your nightly prayer.

Imagine the life you'd build if you spoke to your own soul the way you speak to the people you love.

We forget that self-talk is not just commentary.
It's choreography.
The way you speak teaches your spirit how to move.
Say "I'm trying" long enough and your body will brace for struggle.
Say "I'm learning" and suddenly the world becomes a classroom instead of a courtroom.
Say "I'm broken" and you'll keep searching for the cracks.
Say "I'm becoming" and you'll start noticing the blooming instead.

Healing is a conversation between who you were and who you're ready to be.
A negotiation between the hurt that shaped you and the hope that's trying to lead you forward.
And the only voice with the authority to declare which one wins is yours.

So, speak.
Speak boldly.
Speak kindly.
Speak like someone who believes in resurrection, even if you're still covered in the dust of your last falling-apart.
Tell the truth about your strength until your doubts get tired.
Tell the truth about your worth until your fear gets quiet.
Tell the truth about your future until your past loosens its grip.
Heal thyself by narrating a life that makes room for the parts of you that you once exiled.
By naming your gifts out loud even when your voice shakes.
By choosing stories that lift your chin instead of lowering your spirit.
Because every time you say, "I can grow," you grow.
Every time you say, "I am worthy," you become a little less willing to settle for what harms you.
Every time you say, "I am healing," your body remembers the blueprint of wholeness.
This is the power you carry.

And maybe that is what healing truly is.
Not the absence of pain, but the presence of a new narrator who finally tells the truth.

So, take back the pen.
Take back the mic.
Take back the script.
Speak yourself free.
Speak yourself forward.
And heal thyself.
With the oldest magic you were ever given.
Your own voice, choosing you on purpose.

NOTICING & INTEGRATION

THE STORIES WE INHERIT

Long before we consciously choose our beliefs, we begin collecting stories about who we are.

- What messages about yourself did you hear repeatedly growing up?
- Which of those messages still influence how you think about yourself today?
- Which stories no longer deserve authority over your life?
- On a scale of 1–10, how intentional are you about the way you speak to yourself?
- What would be different if that number were one point higher?

THE VOICE INSIDE

We all have an internal narrator. The question is whether that narrator is helping us grow or keeping us stuck.

- What phrases or thoughts do you find yourself repeating most often?
- How do those words affect the way you show up in your life?
- If your self-talk reflected your deepest values instead of your deepest fears, what might sound different?
- On a scale of 1–10, how supportive is your inner dialogue on most days?
- If you were one point higher on that scale, what is one thing you would say to yourself more often?

BECOMING

This poem suggests that healing is not simply about recovering what was lost. It is about becoming who you are capable of being.

- What version of yourself are you actively growing toward?
- What strengths, values, or qualities are becoming more visible in this season of your life?
- What would change if you viewed yourself as a work in progress rather than a finished product?
- On a scale from 1–10, how much grace do you give yourself while you are still growing?
- If you were one point higher...what expectation, criticism, or pressure would you release as you continue becoming?

WHAT'S ALREADY TRUE

Sometimes growth is not about discovering something new. Sometimes it is about recognizing what has been present all along. The strength you needed may have already been carrying you. The guidance you were seeking may have been quietly unfolding. The truth you're searching for may be something you've known for far longer than you realize.

- What evidence already exists that you are speaking to yourself differently than you once did?
- When have you recently shown yourself grace, patience, or understanding that an earlier version of you might not have offered?
- What strengths, gifts, or qualities have remained present throughout your story, even during your most difficult seasons?

MICRO PRACTICE
REWRITE THE SCRIPT

The words we repeat become the stories we live.

Complete the following:

THE OLD STORY
One message I have carried about myself for too long is ____.

THE TRUTH
A more accurate, compassionate, or empowering truth is ____.

THE EVIDENCE
I know this is true because ____.

THE PRACTICE
When I notice the old story returning, I will remind myself ____.

THE FUTURE
The story I want to continue writing about myself is ____.

CARRY THIS FORWARD

You will speak to yourself thousands of times before this week is over.

The question is not whether you are talking to yourself. The question is whether your words are helping you heal.

Every story has a narrator. Every life has a voice that shapes what comes next. For too many people, that voice becomes an echo of old wounds. Old criticisms. Old fears. Old conclusions that were formed long before they had enough life experience to challenge them.

But you are not obligated to continue repeating a story simply because it has been repeated before. You can question it. You can revise it. You can replace it. Not with fantasy. Not with denial. But with truth.

Healing is not pretending everything is okay. Healing is learning to tell the truth about your strength, your worth, your resilience, and your capacity to grow.

So, pay attention to the words you practice. Because your mind is listening. Your heart is listening. Your future is listening. And every time you choose a story rooted in possibility rather than limitation, you make it easier for the person you are becoming to emerge.

Take back the pen. Tell the truth. And write carefully. You are living your own words every day.

IF THIS BODY WERE BORROWED

Once you begin changing the way you speak to yourself, something unexpected happens.

You start noticing all the other ways you've been treating yourself, too. Because self-talk is never just language. It becomes behavior. It becomes habits. It becomes boundaries. It becomes the daily choices that either reinforce or contradict the story you're trying to write.

For years, many of us learned to evaluate ourselves through performance. How productive we were. How useful we were. How much we could carry. How much we could endure. And somewhere along the way, we began treating our bodies like employees instead of companions. Machines instead of miracles. We demanded output while ignoring maintenance. Expected performance while neglecting restoration. Asked for more while offering very little in return.

It's a strange contradiction. We often extend remarkable compassion toward the people we love. We encourage them to rest. We remind them to eat. We worry when they overwork. We celebrate when they care for themselves. Yet many of us struggle to offer that same grace to the person staring back at us in the mirror. Perhaps because somewhere along the way, we learned that care had to be earned. That rest required permission. That our worth was connected to our usefulness.

But healing asks different questions: "*What if your body is not a project to fix?" "What if it is something to honor?" "What if the same compassion you've been extending to everyone else belongs to you as well?"* Because self-respect is not only reflected in what you think. It is reflected in how you care for what carries you.

The next piece is an invitation to reconsider the relationship you have with the one place you'll spend your entire life. Your body. And the sacred responsibility of caring for it well.

IF THIS BODY WERE BORROWED

Imagine you wake up in the body of the person you love most in the world.
The one whose laughter you memorize.
Whose joy you guard with both hands.
Whose safety you would trade sleep, comfort, and whole seasons of your life to protect.
Imagine God whispers to you: "Take care of this for the next 90 days. Whatever you do to it, they will have to live with when you return it."

Tell the truth...
You would move like a guardian.
You would study nutrition labels like scripture.
You would pour water into that vessel as if hydration were holy work.
You would hunt for vitamins, not vices.
You would let rest be rest instead of punishment or reward.
You would treat movement not as obligation, but as thanksgiving.
Lifting, stretching, walking, sweating like prayer with breath in it.
You would protect that body from exhaustion.
From neglect.
From the slow poison of "I'll start tomorrow."
You would speak to it softly.
Feed it kindly.
Honor it daily.
Because it does not belong to you, and love makes stewardship sacred.

Now here's the twist...
That body is yours.
Always has been.
Always will be.
You are the beloved you keep waiting to prioritize.
The vessel you occupy is yours on consignment.
But we talk to ourselves as if our own ribs don't house anything holy.
We treat our organs like afterthoughts.
Our muscles like strangers.
Our health like a bill we hope never comes due.
We forget that the heart is listening every time we say, "I don't have time."
We forget the body obeys whatever story we repeat long enough.

We forget that longevity isn't luck, it's accumulated care.
Compounded compassion.
Generosity toward the vessel we've been criticizing more than we've been nourishing.

Treat your body the way you'd treat theirs.
Feed it greens.
Not because you "should," but because love deserves fuel.
Lift the weight.
Not because you want abs by summer, but because strength is a language you're finally learning to speak to yourself.
Go for the walk.
Because lungs crave gratitude in the form of oxygen.
Stretch.
Because flexibility is a metaphor for every part of you that deserves to stay open.
Drink the water.
Take the vitamins.
Choose the whole foods.
Honor the sleep.
Schedule the checkups.
Listen to the warning signs.
Treat stress like a hazard light instead of a twisted badge of honor.
Because if you would protect someone else's body with devotion, you can protect your own with the same sincerity.

And here's the deeper truth...
Your body is not an ornament.
It is an instrument.
It is the vehicle for your calling.
The vessel for your joy.
The home for your breath.
The only place you will ever truly live.

So, when you rise tomorrow...
Ask yourself, *"If I were returning this body to someone I deeply love...how would I treat it today?"*
And then treat yourself that way.
Not for 90 days.
Not until the scale approves.

Not until you "earn" care.
But because love is proven in consistency, not conditions.
This body has carried you through storms you never spoke of.
It has survived everything you thought would break it.
It deserves the kind of care you offer everyone else without hesitation.

So, nourish it.
Move it.
Strengthen it.
Restore it.
Bless it.
Thank it.
Care for yourself with the reverence you've been saving for others.
Because this body is borrowed.

NOTICING & INTEGRATION

STEWARDSHIP VS. OWNERSHIP

We often care for others in ways we never consider caring for ourselves. Yet when it comes to our own bodies, we can become dismissive, critical, neglectful, or endlessly demanding.

- If your body truly belonged to someone you deeply loved, what would you do differently today?
- In what ways do you currently care for others more consistently than you care for yourself?
- What assumptions have you inherited about self-care, health, or rest?
- On a scale of 1–10, how well are you currently caring for your body as an act of respect rather than obligation?
- What would you do differently if you were one point higher?

LISTENING TO THE BODY

The body is always communicating. Through energy. Through tension. Through pain. Through fatigue. Many of us have become skilled at overriding those messages. But wisdom often begins with listening.

- What has your body been trying to tell you lately?
- Where do you notice signs of depletion, stress, tension, or fatigue?
- What needs have you been postponing because other responsibilities felt more important?
- On a scale of 1–10, how connected do you currently feel to your body's needs?
- If that number moved one point higher, what would you begin noticing sooner?

CARE AS AN EXPRESSION OF LOVE

Many people wait to care for themselves until they feel worthy. Until they lose the weight. Until they have more time. Until life slows down. But love rarely works that way. Love is practiced before perfection arrives.

- What would change if you treated care as something you deserve?
- What daily habits help you feel most alive, energized, or well?
- How might caring for your body strengthen your ability to show up for your purpose, relationships, and calling?
- On a scale of 1–10, how much do your daily habits communicate respect for the body you live in?
- If that number moved one point higher, what would you do differently this week?

WHAT'S ALREADY TRUE

Your body has already carried you through more than you sometimes acknowledge. It has survived stress, grief, uncertainty, disappointment, healing, growth, and change. Even now, it continues showing up for you in ways that deserve recognition.

- What evidence already exists that your body has been resilient, adaptable, and stronger than you sometimes give it credit for?
- What healthy habits, routines, or practices are you already maintaining that deserve appreciation rather than criticism?
- What changes when you view caring for your body not as punishment or self-improvement, but as gratitude?

MICRO PRACTICE

THE 24-HOUR STEWARDSHIP EXPERIMENT

For the next 24 hours, imagine your body belongs to someone you deeply love.

Not someone you are responsible for fixing. Someone you are responsible for caring for. As you move through the day, pause before major decisions involving food, rest, movement, stress, or recovery.

Ask yourself:

"If this body belonged to someone I deeply loved, what would I choose right now?"

Notice what comes to mind...then do the things!

Would you drink the water?
Would you take the walk?
Would you get the sleep?
Would you eat differently?
Would you speak more kindly?
Would you allow yourself to rest?

At the end of the day, reflect on the following:

What felt different?
What surprised me?
What did I realize about the way I normally treat myself?
What is one practice I want to carry forward?

Then, complete this sentence:

"Tomorrow, I will care for my body by ____."

Keep it simple.
Keep it realistic.
Keep it repeatable.

Because stewardship is not built through dramatic decisions.
It is built through daily acts of care.

CARRY THIS FORWARD

Your body is not your enemy. It is not a project. It is not a punishment. It is not an obstacle standing between you and the life you want. It is the vehicle carrying you there. The vessel through which you love. Serve. Work. Create. Laugh. Pray. Heal. And become.

This body has carried you through storms you rarely talk about. It has survived things that once convinced you they might break you. It has adapted. Recovered. Endured. And continued showing up.

Perhaps it deserves more gratitude than criticism. More partnership than punishment. More compassion than condemnation. The goal is not perfection. The goal is stewardship.

To nourish what nourishes you. To strengthen what supports you. To honor what carries you. Not because a number on a scale says you are worthy. Not because you have finally earned care. Not because you have become someone different. Because you are already worthy of the same kindness you offer everyone else.

So feed it. Move it. Rest it. Strengthen it. Listen to it. Thank it. And remember: Love is not only expressed through what you give away. Love looks like caring for the body that has been carrying you all along.

FULL CUP, EMPTY BATTERY

Caring for yourself is bigger than nutrition labels, gym memberships, step counts, and annual checkups.

Those things matter. But they are only part of the story. Because there is another form of stewardship many of us overlook. The stewardship of energy. The stewardship of attention. The stewardship of capacity.

Most of us learn to recognize physical exhaustion. The aching muscles. The heavy eyelids. The need for sleep. But emotional exhaustion is quieter. Mental fatigue is subtler. Spiritual depletion often disguises itself as irritability, numbness, impatience, cynicism, or the strange feeling of being surrounded by people while somehow feeling absent from yourself.

And perhaps that is because many of us have become extraordinarily skilled at giving. Giving our time. Giving our attention. Giving our care. Giving our wisdom. Giving our presence. Giving until generosity quietly becomes depletion. Giving until compassion becomes fatigue. Giving until our batteries are blinking red while our smiles still convince everyone we're fine.

The challenge is that being needed can feel meaningful. Helping can feel purposeful. Showing up can feel noble. Until one day you realize you've been pouring from a well that hasn't been replenished in far too long.

The goal is not to become less generous. The goal is to become sustainable. Because even the brightest light requires a power source. Even the fullest cup has limits. Even the most loving heart requires restoration.

The next piece is for anyone who has ever felt deeply fulfilled and deeply exhausted at the same time. Anyone who has ever discovered that a full cup and an empty battery can coexist. And anyone learning that rest is not retreat. It's stewardship.

FULL CUP, EMPTY BATTERY

There's a strange math to my spirit...
How I can hold so much love in my chest that it spills over the rim,
yet feel my energy evaporates faster than a puddle in August heat.
I adore connection.
Warmth. Laughter.
The way good energy tilts the world back into balance.
I love affection.
Alignment. Resonance.
That soft click when spirits find their matching frequency.
But even joy runs a current.
Even joy draws power.
You stay plugged into too many people for too long, and eventually the signal flickers.
The screen dims.
The body whispers, "sit down."

I'm an extroverted introvert, which is just a poetic way of saying
I shine brightly...but not indefinitely.
My soul has a charging port, not an infinite power supply.
I can pour into a room until the whole atmosphere feels held.
Until everyone's shoulders drop an inch.
Until tension dissolves like sugar in warm tea.
But afterward?
I'm in a corner somewhere quietly melting.
performing emotional CPR on myself with silence and snacks.

People see the full cup and assume the battery matches it.
But those are separate systems.
One can overflow while the other is blinking red.
We panic when our phones hit ten percent.
But when our bodies hit ten percent, we say, "I'm good."
As if exhaustion must be theatrical to be believed.
As if peace requires permission slips.

The truth is simple...
My body knows when the world has had enough of me for the day.
My mind knows when its edges are fraying.
My spirit knows when its light is thinning.

Pulling itself inward the way a tide retreats.
Not out of cruelty, out of necessity.
And so, sometimes I disappear.
Not dramatically, just deliberately.
Twenty-four hours of quiet is not a crisis...
It is a cure.
It is me letting my nervous system uncurl itself.
Letting my thoughts unclench.
Letting my heartbeat remember it is not a drumline.

I don't vanish because I'm fragile.
I vanish because I'm trying to be faithful.
Faithful to my own humanity,
Faithful to the truth that I cannot love deeply if I am running on spiritual fumes.
Rest is not indulgence.
It is infrastructure.
It is the scaffolding that keeps compassion upright.
When I ignore that, even kindness becomes heavy.
Even empathy begins to echo.
Even joy starts to feel like something I owe instead of something I enjoy.
Solitude is not my escape...
it is my recalibration.
My soft reboot.
My manual override when life overloads the circuit.

I am learning to honor every flicker of my inner flame.
I am learning to say, "I love you... and I need a minute,"
Before fatigue turns my kindness sharp.
Before overstimulation rewrites my tone.
Before I morph into a version of myself that even I don't recognize.

Joy fills me.
Joy also empties me.
Love expands me.
Love also requires energy to metabolize.
Even when the people are good.
Even when the connection is beautiful.
Even when the room feels like home.

So, I'm building rhythms now.
Recharge.
Reset.
Return.
Touch soil.
Drink water.
Let silence braid itself back into my bones.
Let solitude sift the noise from the signal.

I'm done apologizing for tending to the machinery that makes me human.
If you see me step away...
Know it is not distance, its devotion.
Not avoidance, alignment.
Not rejection, maintenance.

Because generosity has limits.
Full cup.
Empty battery.
Both can be true at once.
Both deserve care.
And I am finally learning to honor them equally.

NOTICING & INTEGRATION

CAPACITY & ENERGY

Many of us measure our capacity by what we can endure. We pride ourselves on showing up, pushing through, and carrying more than seems reasonable. Productivity can become proof of worth.

- What situations, people, or responsibilities tend to drain your energy most quickly?
- How do you typically know when your emotional, mental, or physical battery is running low?
- What messages did you learn about rest, productivity, or self-care?
- On a scale of 1–10, how aware are you of your energy levels before you become exhausted?
- If you were one point higher, what would you recognize sooner?

GIVING & RECEIVING

Sometimes we become so committed to showing up for others that we stop noticing what it costs us. We continue giving long after our battery has entered the red.

- How do you know the difference between healthy generosity and overextension?
- Where in your life are you consistently pouring without replenishing?
- What support, care, or nourishment have you struggled to receive from others?
- On a scale of 1–10, how balanced do you currently feel between giving and receiving?
- If that number moved one point higher, what would change?

REST & PERMISSION

Rest is often misunderstood. Many people treat rest as a reward for productivity rather than a requirement for sustainability. Others wait until burnout forces them to stop. But rest is not weakness. It is maintenance.

- What makes it difficult for you to rest without guilt?
- What would become possible if you treated rest as stewardship rather than indulgence?
- What routines help you feel restored, grounded, and fully yourself?
- On a scale of 1–10, how much permission do you currently give yourself to rest before you are exhausted?
- If that number moved one point higher, what would you begin doing differently?

WHAT'S ALREADY TRUE

You have likely already learned more about your needs than you realize. Your body has been sending signals. Your mind has been offering clues. Your spirit has been trying to teach you what restoration looks like.

- What are you already doing that helps you recharge, even in small ways?
- When have you noticed yourself honoring your limits instead of ignoring them? What happened?
- In what ways, even small, do you see evidence that you are capable of protecting your energy?

MICRO PRACTICE
BATTERY CHECK

Most of us regularly check our phones. Few of us regularly check ourselves. Today, pause and perform a battery check.

Draw four categories on a page:

Physical
Mental
Relational
Professional

For each area, answer the below questions:

What is currently charging me?
What is currently draining me?
What have I been tolerating that is costing more than it deserves?
What am I needing more of right now?

Now complete the following:

"My battery is not low because I am weak. My battery is low because I have been carrying ____."

"The next act of stewardship I can offer myself is ____."

Then choose one small action.

Take the nap.
Go for the walk.
Drink the water.
Turn off the notifications.
Say no.
Go home.
Sit quietly.
Whatever your battery is asking for, honor it.
Not tomorrow.
Today.

CARRY THIS FORWARD

You are allowed to be full of love and low on energy at the same time. You are allowed to care deeply and still need space. You are allowed to enjoy people and still need solitude. You are allowed to give generously and still require replenishment.

These truths do not compete with one another. They complete one another. The goal is not to become less caring. The goal is to become more sustainable.

Because even joy requires energy. Even purpose requires recovery. Even fire requires fuel. You were never designed to operate at maximum output indefinitely. You were designed for rhythm. For cycles. For seasons of pouring and seasons of replenishing. For connection and solitude. For contribution and restoration.

So, stop waiting until you are depleted to listen. Stop treating exhaustion as proof that you care enough. Stop apologizing for tending to the systems that make your life possible. Your battery deserves the same attention your cup receives.

Because a full cup means little if there is no energy left to carry it. Rest before resentment. Recharge before collapse. Reset before burnout.

And remember: Stepping away is not abandonment, It is stewardship. Not avoidance, alignment. Not rejection, maintenance.

Even God rested.

FINDING MY VOICE

There is something remarkable that happens when you stop spending all of your energy surviving. You begin hearing yourself again.

Not the version of you shaped by expectations. Not the version of you performing competence. Not the version of you trying to be everything for everyone. The real one. The one whose thoughts arrive before they are edited. The one whose dreams appear before practicality talks them out of existence. The one who remembers what matters without needing anyone else's approval to validate it.

Perhaps that is one of the hidden gifts of rest. Rest creates space. And space has a way of revealing things. Truths you've been too busy to hear. Desires you've been too exhausted to pursue. Parts of yourself you've been translating for so long that you've forgotten how they sound in their original language.

For many people, losing their voice doesn't happen all at once. It's gradual. A compromise here. A swallowed truth there. A moment of shrinking to stay safe. A decision to remain silent because speaking felt costly. Until eventually, the voice is still there... But buried. Waiting. Patiently.

The journey back to ourselves requires more than healing. More than rest. More than self-care. It requires expression. Because a truth that is never spoken remains trapped. A gift that is never shared remains wrapped. A voice that is never used slowly begins to believe it was never meant to exist.

The next piece is about reclaiming that voice. Not the polished version. Not the acceptable version. Not the version that makes everyone comfortable. The real one. The one that survived every attempt to silence it. The one that has been waiting all along. To be heard.

FINDING MY VOICE

I was taught that children should be seen, not heard.
So, I learned to fold my words into silence.
Like letters never mailed.
Dreams left crumpled in the back pocket of hand-me-down jeans.
"Go to your room."
"Read a book."
Punishment was always exile.
And if the first cut was banishment, the second cut was the book report.
How sad...
To be told that language was labor.
That thought was punishment.

But that punishment produced a poet.
That exile made an advocate.
That silence trained my lungs to carry sound like prophecy.

I spent years swallowing my words.
Listening to voices outside of me.
Shutting down the one that mattered most.
I shrank myself because my body already took up too much space.
Quieted myself because my presence was already too loud.

But God had other plans.
Because armor isn't forged in ease.
It's built in fire.
In fracture.
In trial.
And the armor He gave me came piece by piece.

The day my clothes were mocked in the hallway...
A shield.
The night my brother didn't come home...
A breastplate.
The moment I realized my Black skin was seen as a threat...
Greaves on my shins.
When my father took his last breath, just 29 days after the VA told him his lungs had been cursed in Vietnam...
Chain mail.

Every rejection...
Every closed door...
Every, "you're so well spoken"...
Every microaggression.
"I don't even see you as Black"...
Meant to be a compliment, but cutting deep with a precision reserved only for the most potent of privileged rhetoric.
Every whispered, "you don't belong here"...
A heavier helmet.
Until the weight itself became a workout.

But what is the point of armor if you never see battle?
What is the point of strength if you've never had to stand?
What does it mean to be undefeated if you've never been tested?
Zero losses sounds amazing.
But sitting next to zero victories...
All you have is nothing.
Resilience has a strange way of repurposing what was meant to diminish you.
Everything they tried to make smaller became material.
The silence became listening.
The listening became observation.
The observation became understanding.
And understanding eventually demanded language.
What they intended as restriction became preparation.
What they called discipline became rehearsal.
Every dismissal taught me something about power.
Every rejection taught me something about persistence.
Every closed door forced me to become more acquainted with the architecture of my own conviction.

I stopped asking permission to exist at full volume.
I stopped mistaking accommodation for belonging.
I stopped translating myself into versions that made other people comfortable.
And somewhere along the way, I realized that what I had always interpreted as weakness was actually capacity.
The capacity to endure.
The capacity to notice.

The capacity to feel deeply without surrendering completely.
The capacity to turn pain into meaning.
Meaning into purpose.

But you can't fold forever.
You can't bow always.
Eventually, even silence cracks.
And when it cracks, sound spills out like light through stained glass.
Now I write.
I speak.
Sometimes, I even sing.
Because once you find your gift, you can't hoard it.
Gifts aren't meant to stay wrapped.
You pass them forward.
Like socks and alarms clocks at Christmas.

I spent years treating my voice like contraband.
Something powerful enough to possess but too dangerous to display.
Years believing that speaking up would cost me safety.
That honesty would cost me belonging.
That authenticity would cost me acceptance.
And to be fair, sometimes it did.
But eventually I learned that silence carries a cost as well.
A cost measured in abandoned dreams.
In unrealized purpose.
In conversations that never happen because someone was waiting for permission that was never coming.

So, I stopped trying to become smaller.
Stopped apologizing for the space I occupy.
Stopped treating my perspective like an interruption instead of a contribution.
Because every scar had already become instruction.
Every setback had already become curriculum.
Every chapter I wished I could skip had already become part of the story that taught me how to tell stories.

They tried to bury my voice.
What they didn't realize was that voices are seeds.
And seeds understand something about darkness.

They know how to grow there.

Now that I've found my voice,
I can't shut up.
And I won't.
Not now.
Not ever.
Because when you find out you were born to speak...
Silence becomes the only sin.
And I will never be seen, and not heard, again.

NOTICING & INTEGRATION

SILENCE & SURVIVAL

Many of us learn, consciously or unconsciously, that certain parts of ourselves are safer when hidden.

- What messages did you receive growing up about speaking up, taking up space, or expressing yourself?
- In what situations do you still find yourself becoming smaller, quieter, or less visible than you would like to be?
- What have those strategies helped you survive, and what might they be costing you now?
- On a scale of 1–10, how comfortable are you expressing your thoughts, needs, and perspectives authentically?
- What would being one-point higher change about your life?

THE STORIES YOU CARRY

The experiences that shape us often become stories we tell ourselves about who we are and what is possible.

- What challenges or setbacks have shaped the way you see yourself?
- Which parts of your story have become sources of strength, wisdom, or resilience?
- What chapter of your life are you beginning to interpret differently than you once did?
- On a scale of 1–10, how much do you view your life experiences as assets rather than liabilities?
- What would it mean for that number to be one point higher?

VOICE, PURPOSE & CONTRIBUTION

Finding your voice is not simply about speaking. It is about becoming willing to contribute what only you can contribute.

- Where in your life do you feel most able to show up fully as yourself?
- What perspective, gift, or insight do you possess that others may benefit from hearing?
- What would become possible if you stopped waiting for permission to be who you already are?
- On a scale of 1–10, how willing are you to share your gifts, perspectives, and contributions without waiting for permission from others?
- If you were one point higher...what conversation, contribution, or act of courage would you stop postponing?

WHAT'S ALREADY TRUE

Not everything you need is ahead of you. Some of it may already be here. The voice you are searching for may not be something you need to find. It may be something you need to trust. The impact you hope to have may already be visible in ways you have overlooked. Sometimes the greatest challenge is not discovering your gifts, but recognizing how they have been developing through every experience that shaped you.

- What evidence already exists that your voice has had a positive impact on someone else?
- When have you spoken up, shared honestly, or shown up authentically and been glad that you did?
- What strengths have been developing beneath the surface through every challenge, rejection, or setback you have endured?

MICRO PRACTICE
THE VOICE AUDIT

Your voice is more than what you say. It is how you show up.

Complete the following:

WHAT I HAVE BEEN QUIET ABOUT

One thing I have been hesitant to say, share, or acknowledge is ________.

WHAT I KNOW

A truth I know but do not always express is ____.

WHAT I BRING

The perspective, gift, or strength I bring into the world is ____.

WHAT I NO LONGER NEED

I no longer need permission to ____.

WHAT I WILL PRACTICE

This week, I will use my voice by ____.

CARRY THIS FORWARD

Finding your voice is not about becoming louder. It is about becoming more honest. More aligned. More willing to stand in the fullness of who you are.

The world will always offer reasons to shrink. To blend in. To wait. To edit yourself into a version that feels more acceptable. But every time you choose authenticity over performance, contribution over concealment, and truth over fear, you reclaim a piece of yourself.

Your voice does not have to be perfect. It does not have to convince everyone. It does not have to be polished before it is worthy. It simply has to be yours. Because the things that shaped you were never meant to silence you.

They were preparing you. And what was planted in darkness was never meant to stay buried. It was meant to grow.

So, speak. Share. Contribute. Not because you have something to prove. But because there is something only you can say. And the world may be waiting to hear it.

I ONLY JUST MET MYSELF

Finding your voice changes things.

Not because the world suddenly listens. Not because every room becomes welcoming. Not because every truth is received the way it deserves to be. Finding your voice changes things because once you've heard yourself clearly, it becomes much harder to pretend you don't know who you are. Who you're becoming.

But there is a strange challenge that often follows self-expression. Many of us spend years learning how to advocate. How to achieve. How to lead. How to perform. How to contribute. How to become known. And somewhere in the process, we become fluent in presenting ourselves without ever fully knowing ourselves.

We learn how to answer the question: *"What do you do?"* Long before we learn how to answer the question: *"Who are you?"* The difference seems subtle. Until life removes the title. The role. The position. The accomplishment. The identity you've spent years introducing before your actual self. Then suddenly you're standing face-to-face with a version of yourself you've rarely had time to meet. Not because they were hidden. Because they were waiting. Waiting beneath the deadlines. Beneath the expectations. Beneath the constant pressure to produce. Waiting for a moment when usefulness would no longer be mistaken for worth.

For many people, this is one of the most disorienting experiences imaginable. And one of the most sacred. Because there comes a moment when you realize that becoming yourself may require grieving the identities that once helped you survive. The roles. The labels. The costumes. The introductions. Not because they were bad. But because they were never meant to carry the full weight of who you are.

The next piece explores what happens when achievement steps aside. When the applause quiets. When the title no longer speaks first. And for the very first time, you are left alone with yourself. Not the résumé. Not the reputation. Just the person. The one you've been becoming all along.

I ONLY JUST MET MYSELF

They threw me a retirement party when I left.
Thirty-three years old.
A lifetime achievement award...
A lifetime?
I still have sneakers from high school.
I still Google recipes for salmon.

They meant it as love.
But it hit like loss.
Because when I walked away from that job.
It didn't just feel like leaving work.
It felt like death.
Like burying a version of me that never learned how to rest in peace.
I built a temple from that title.
Rolled it around my tongue like scripture.
Every syllable tasted like sacrifice.
I wore the responsibility...
Until I realized the crown was a chain.
I didn't know where the job ended and I began.
Didn't know how to introduce myself without the org attached to my name.
Didn't know how to not follow "hello" with an elevator pitch or mission statement.

I spent years confusing visibility with value.
Recognition for relationship.
Admiration for affection.
Applause for affirmation.
Building my identity from borrowed reflections and calling it self-awareness.
Handing strangers a ballot for an election God never intended them to participate in.

Every room became a stage.
Every introduction became a performance.
Every interaction became an opportunity to represent something other than myself.
The organization needed a leader.

The community needed an advocate.
The board needed confidence.
The donors needed reassurance.
And somewhere in the process, I became fluent in being needed.
So fluent, in fact, that I forgot how to simply be.

I forgot that worth and usefulness are not synonyms.
Forgot that purpose and productivity are not the same thing.
Forgot that God never asked me to become a machine.
Only faithful.
And faithfulness looks very different from exhaustion.
Very different from burnout.
Very different from sacrificing yourself so completely that e people applauding your work can no longer see the person doing it.

And when COVID hit...
For the first time, I didn't have to put the armor on.
Could log in from the chest up.
Could let my sweatpants breathe.
Could start to meet the me that lived underneath the press release.
That season felt strange.
Like being alone with a stranger who looked a lot like me but talked about dreams I never pursued.
Who wanted to sleep without guilt.
Eat without multitasking,
Laugh without turning it into outreach.
Then came the silence.
The phone that used to ring nonstop...
Contracts...
Calls...
Calendars...
Went quiet.

I realized I didn't miss the work.
I missed the witnesses.
I missed being needed.
I missed being noticed.
Because when the world only knows you for what you give, who checks in when you stop giving?

A friend used to tell me "I can't wait for you to show up at my house with a hole in your sock."
I didn't recognize that statement for the prophecy that it was at the time.

The strange thing about stepping away is that nobody warns you how quiet it gets.
Not the absence of work.
The absence of validation.
The absence of being the person everyone calls.
The absence of urgency.
Because urgency has a way of masquerading as significance.
And when it disappears, you are forced to confront a difficult question...
If nobody needs anything from me today, who am I?

That question terrified me.
Because for years my identity had been stitched together from usefulness.
From output.
From impact.
From the ability to solve problems and carry weight and keep moving no matter how tired I became.

Life handed me the gift I didn't realize I needed...Stillness.
Enough stillness to notice my own reflection.
Enough stillness to recognize that beneath every title was a person I had not spent nearly enough time getting to know.
A man who liked things I had forgotten.
A man who was tired.
A man who was breaking.
A man who had never actually learned how to introduce himself.

And maybe that was the real work all along.
Not building a career.
Not building an organization.
Not building a reputation.
Building a relationship with the person God entrusted me to become.
Finding yourself sounds beautiful until you start digging.
Because under every title is a truth you buried to wear it.
Under every success is a scar that never got to heal.
And when you strip it all down there's not applause waiting.

There's quiet.
And quiet is loud when you've been running your whole life.

I started binge-watching old shows.
The ones that used to play in the background while I worked through midnight emails.
It was like meeting my old self through secondhand stories.
I laughed at jokes I never heard before.
Felt sadness I never gave myself permission for.
It was humbling...
And holy.

There was a time when I needed the uniform.
Needed the title.
Needed the introduction.
Needed the room to tell me who I was before I could believe it myself.
I still wear suits.
But now they're just fabric.
Functional.
Because confidence no longer hangs in my closet.
It lives somewhere deeper.
Somewhere beyond achievement.
Beyond reputation.
Beyond performance.
It lives in the quiet certainty that I am no less valuable on my day off than I was on my busiest day.
No less worthy when the phone is silent.
No less significant when nobody is applauding.

I spent years introducing myself through what I did.
Now I am learning how to introduce myself through who I am.
And that has changed everything.
Because titles expire.
Organizations evolve.
Careers end.
Reputations shift.
But purpose survives all of it.
Purpose is what remains when every costume is returned to wardrobe.
When every role has taken its final bow.

When every business card has been recycled.
Purpose is the part of you God recognized before the world ever learned your name.
And for the first time in a very long time, I am no longer trying to become someone.
And that feels a lot like freedom.

When they ask me, "So what do you do now?"
I tell them, "I'm doing me."
Because I've realized, I didn't lose my calling.
I shed my costume.
I thought walking away was failure.
But it was baptism.
I thought I lost my purpose.
But I found myself.
And he was worth meeting.
And beneath it all, I found God waiting.
Arms open.
Whispering...
"Welcome home. You've been busy."

NOTICING & INTEGRATION

BEYOND THE ROLE

Many of us spend years becoming successful at roles we never stop to examine.

- What roles, titles, or identities have been most important in shaping how you see yourself?
- How much of your self-worth is connected to what you do versus who you are?
- If those roles disappeared tomorrow, what parts of you would remain?
- On a scale of 1–10, how strongly is your sense of value tied to your productivity, achievements, or usefulness?
- If that number were one point higher, what would be different?

THE COST OF BEING NEEDED

Being needed can feel meaningful. It can also become a place to hide.

- In what ways have you become accustomed to being needed by others?
- What emotions surface when things become quiet, slow, or still?
- What have you learned about yourself during seasons when external validation was less available?
- On a scale of 1–10, how comfortable are you simply being, without needing to prove, produce, or perform?
- What would be different if that number were one point higher?

MEETING YOURSELF

This poem suggests that the most important relationship we build is the one we have with ourselves.

- What have you discovered about yourself during periods of transition, stillness, or change?
- What interests, dreams, joys, or parts of yourself have been waiting for your attention?
- What does the version of you beneath the title, position, or accomplishment want you to know?
- On a scale of 1–10, how well do you feel you know yourself apart from your roles, responsibilities, and accomplishments?
- If you were just one point higher, what would you make more time, space, or attention for in your life?

WHAT'S ALREADY TRUE

Not everything you need is ahead of you. Some of it may already be here. For many of us, the search for identity becomes tangled with achievement, responsibility, and the roles we play for others. We become so accustomed to introducing ourselves through what we do that we rarely pause to ask who we are beneath it all. Sometimes the most important discovery is realizing that your worth has been present all along, waiting patiently beneath the titles, expectations, and accomplishments that once defined you.

- What evidence already exists that your value extends far beyond what you produce or accomplish?
- When have you felt most alive, connected, or fulfilled in ways that had nothing to do with achievement or recognition?
- What parts of yourself have remained present and worthy through every chapter, regardless of the title you carried?

MICRO PRACTICE
THE INTRODUCTION

For many of us, introductions begin with what we do. This exercise invites you to explore who you are beneath the role.

Complete the following:

BEYOND THE TITLE
If I could not describe myself using my job, accomplishments, or responsibilities, I would say I am someone who ____.

WHAT MATTERS MOST
The qualities I value most about myself are ____.

WHAT I ENJOY
Something I genuinely enjoy, simply because it brings me joy, is ____.

WHAT REMAINS
No matter what changes in my life, ____ remains true about who I am.

A NEW INTRODUCTION
Write a new introduction for yourself beginning with:

"I am someone who..."

CARRY THIS FORWARD

There is nothing wrong with achievement. There is nothing wrong with meaningful work. There is nothing wrong with being useful.

The danger begins when those things become the only evidence we allow ourselves to use when measuring our worth. Because eventually every title changes. Every role evolves. Every season ends. And when it does, the question becomes: Who remains?

The answer cannot be your position. It cannot be your productivity. It cannot be your reputation. Those things are temporary. They are roles you play. Not the entirety of who you are.

Real freedom begins when you recognize your identity is larger than your résumé. When your worth survives a day off. When your value survives stillness. When your sense of self no longer depends on applause, urgency, or accomplishment.

The goal was never to become indispensable. The goal was always to become whole. So, spend time with the person beneath the title. The one beneath the performance. The one beneath the expectation.

You may discover that the person you've been searching for has been there all along. Waiting patiently to be introduced.

FALLEN LEAVES

Meeting yourself is beautiful. It is also inconvenient.

Because once you begin seeing yourself clearly, it becomes difficult to ignore everything that no longer fits. The habits. The roles. The relationships. The expectations. The stories you inherited and never consciously chose. Self-discovery has a way of creating a new kind of tension. Not because you've become confused. Because you've become aware. And awareness changes everything.

Once you recognize the difference between who you are and who you've been pretending to be, the gap becomes impossible to ignore. You begin noticing where you're performing instead of living. Where you're accommodating instead of aligning. Where you're holding onto things not because they're healthy, but because they're familiar. And familiarity can be powerful. Even when it's painful. Especially when it's painful.

The truth is, many of the things we eventually outgrow once served a purpose. They protected us. Helped us survive. Helped us belong. Helped us make sense of seasons we weren't fully equipped to navigate. The challenge is that survival tools often overstay their welcome. What once protected us can eventually restrict us. What once provided safety can eventually prevent growth. What once fit can eventually become too small.

And yet, letting go is rarely immediate. Rarely clean. Rarely easy. Because part of us remembers how much those things once mattered. How much they once helped. How much of ourselves became attached to them. Growth is often described as adding something new. New skills. New opportunities. New perspectives. But some of the most important growth you'll ever experience is subtractive. It arrives through release. Through shedding. Through trusting that what is leaving is not always being lost. Sometimes it is simply making room.

The next piece is about that sacred process. The quiet courage required to loosen your grip. To trust the season. And to honor the truth that not everything meant to serve your growth was meant to stay forever.

FALLEN LEAVES

I went walking today.
Feet in rhythm with the wind.
Kicking through leaves like shattering panes in a window made of everything I used to be.
Each a version of me that thought survival was strength.
That thought armor was beautiful.
The ground is covered in yesterday's stories, but I'm still standing.
Bare, but whole.
Because the truth is, I don't need adornment to prove I'm alive.
There was a time when every step sounded like loss.
Like something behind me breaking under the weight of my becoming.
The crunch wasn't subtle.
It didn't whisper.
It announced itself.
It was sharp.
Undeniable.
Like memory refusing to be ignored.

But I learned to listen differently.
That sound wasn't grief, it was growth.
It was the past making room.
Because every leaf that fell carried a version of me that could not follow where I was being called.
And I didn't always release it gracefully.
Some things I held onto out of habit.
Some out of fear.
Some because I had convinced myself that survival required preservation.
That if I let too much go, there would be nothing left of me to recognize.
Unchanging on the surface, even as everything inside me was frozen.
I tried to manufacture spring before I had honored the winter.
Tried to bloom without first being still.

But you can't rush seasons that were designed to teach you something.
Letting go is not a form of dying. It is a form of trusting.
Trusting that what is leaving is not being taken but released. Trusting that absence can be intentional.
That space is not emptiness, it is preparation.

Because the soul needs room to expand into what it's becoming.
Not as something delicate, but as something living.
Something that knows how to take light and turn it into life.
Even when that light hits a wound first.
Especially then.

Because there is something sacred about what happens when love meets what was once broken and refuses to leave it that way.
That's not fragility.
That's transformation.
I am not less than I was. I am refined.
Stripped of what could not sustain me.
Freed from what could not follow me.
And yes, there are moments where the branches feel bare.
Where I look around and don't recognize the landscape of my own life.
But the roots, the roots are steady.
Deeper than they've ever been.
Aligned in a way that no storm has been able to undo.

As I walk, I watch trees undress with dignity.
Even the mighty maple knows you can't hold on to everything and still reach toward heaven.
See, I thought the leaves were protecting me.
But they were only a facade.
As was the trunk.
My strength lied in the roots.
Roots I can't see but that are the only thing that can bring real nourishment.
I know the leaves will come back.
Not as what was, but as what's next.
They'll look different.
In the shape of surrender.
The hue of hope that covered me when I breaking..
And I'll smile.
Knowing God didn't take, He traded.
Didn't silence, He saved.
Didn't end, He expanded.

NOTICING & INTEGRATION

IDENTITY & SHEDDING

We may assume that if something helped us survive, we are obligated to keep it. But not every version of you was built for every season. Some were necessary for then, but too small for now.

- What version of yourself are you currently outgrowing?
- What beliefs or narratives once helped you survive but may no longer serve who you are becoming?
- What are you still holding onto simply because it feels familiar?
- On a scale of 1–10, how ready are you to let go of what no longer serves you?
- What would be different if you were just one point higher?

PROTECTION & LIMITATION

Sometimes armor protects what is tender. Sometimes it gives us enough structure to keep standing. But when protection becomes permanent, it can harden into distance, control, avoidance, or isolation.

- What has been your armor, and how has it helped you?
- In what ways might that same armor now be preventing connection, growth, or peace?
- What would it feel like to set it down, even briefly?
- On a scale of 1–10, how much do you trust that you can be safe without relying on old protective patterns?
- What keeps you at that level and not lower on the scale?

TRUSTING THE CYCLE

Leaves fall because trees know something we often forget. Not every loss is punishment. Sometimes what falls away creates the very space needed for what comes next to grow.

- What are you afraid will happen if you let go?
- Where have you seen in your life that endings made room for new beginnings?
- What might be trying to grow in your life right now, but does not yet have enough space?
- On a scale of 1–10, how much do you trust that something meaningful can grow in the space created by release?
- If that number moved one point higher, what would you stop trying to hold together?

WHAT'S ALREADY TRUE

You have already survived seasons of change. You have already released things you once thought you could not live without. You have already witnessed endings that eventually revealed themselves as openings.

- What are you already doing that suggests you are outgrowing the version of yourself that is no longer aligned with the future you are building?
- Where in your life have you already let go of something and created space for something better, healthier, or more honest?
- What shifts when you trust that nothing truly meant for you will require you to shrink in order to keep it?

MICRO PRACTICE
WRITE, NAME, RELEASE

Letting go becomes more powerful when we stop treating it like vague emotion and begin naming what is actually ready to be released. This practice is about honoring what helped you survive while telling the truth about what no longer needs to define you.

Find a quiet space.
Take a few slow breaths.
Choose one belief, role, behavior, expectation, or relationship pattern that you feel ready to release.

Write it clearly at the top of the page, then complete the following:

NAME WHAT IT WAS

The thing I am ready to release is ____.

It once helped me by ____.

I understand why I needed it then because ____.

NAME WHAT IT COSTS

It is now limiting me by ____.

When I continue holding onto it, I notice ____.

The part of me that is ready to grow needs ____.

NAME WHAT COMES NEXT

I release this with gratitude, not because it failed me, but because I have outgrown it.

In its place, I am making room for ____.

The next version of me is asking for ____.

MAKE IT PHYSICAL

When you are finished, choose one symbolic action.

You may tear the page. Crumple it. Fold it and place it somewhere meaningful. Safely discard it.
Or keep it as a record of what you are choosing to release.
The action matters less than the intention.
Let your body participate in the decision your spirit is making.

CARRY THIS FORWARD

You are not being stripped. You are being refined. There is a difference.

Being stripped suggests loss without purpose. Refinement suggests that something essential is being revealed. Sometimes what falls away is not being taken from you. Sometimes it is being removed because it cannot survive where you are going next.

Old armor. Old stories. Old definitions of strength. Old versions of belonging that required you to become smaller than your spirit was willing to remain.

It is natural to grieve what you are outgrowing. Even when release is right, it can still be tender. Even when you know something no longer fits, there may still be a part of you that remembers when it protected you. Honor that.

Do not shame the version of you that needed what you no longer need. Thank them. Bless them. Then keep becoming. Because release is not rejection. Release is recognition. Recognition that the season has changed. Recognition that the roots are still intact. Recognition that what falls is not always failure. Sometimes it is preparation. So do not rush to replace what leaves. Do not panic in the space that opens.

Stand there. Bare. Honest. Rooted. Let the empty branches remind you that visibility is not vulnerability when your roots are deep. What is falling away was never meant to go where you are going next. And what grows next may not look like what was.

It may look more like who you are becoming.

I FORGIVE YOU, BUT I RELEASE YOU

Some things are easier to release than others.

A habit. An outdated belief. A version of yourself you've outgrown. Those losses can be painful. But they often make sense. Relationships are different. Because people are not simply part of our story. They become woven into it. Their voices shape our inner dialogue. Their presence becomes part of our routines. Their approval becomes part of our confidence. Their absence becomes part of our grief.

And perhaps that is why some of the heaviest things we carry are not objects, responsibilities, or expectations. They are relationships that no longer fit the life we are trying to build. Relationships that once brought comfort but now bring confusion. Relationships that once felt reciprocal but now feel one-sided. Relationships that require us to abandon ourselves in order to preserve them.

The difficult truth is that love and alignment are not always the same thing. You can love someone deeply and still recognize that their presence in your life comes at too great a cost. You can appreciate what a relationship once was and still acknowledge what it has become. You can honor the history without sacrificing your future.

Many of us were taught that forgiveness means reconciliation. That love requires unlimited access. That loyalty demands self-abandonment. But healing often teaches a different lesson.

Sometimes forgiveness is not an invitation back in. Sometimes forgiveness is simply the decision to stop carrying the weight. To stop replaying the argument. To stop negotiating with reality. To stop waiting for someone to become who they have repeatedly shown you they are not prepared to become. Because release is not revenge. It is clarity. And clarity is one of the most compassionate gifts we can offer ourselves.

The next piece explores a truth many people spend years resisting: You can forgive someone. You can love someone. You can wish them well. And still decide they no longer have access to your peace.

I FORGIVE YOU, BUT I RELEASE YOU

I learned the difference between forgiveness and access lying in a hospital bed.
Watching my body negotiate with survival in real time.
Blood trying to remember its boundaries.
Machines speaking in soft alarms and measured mercy.
Nurses moving with the calm of people who have seen God up close and learned not to stare.
I was there for five days. Four nights.
Multiple transfusions. A body emptied and refilled.
A spirit thinned enough to hear clearly.
That's where the lesson arrived.
Not dramatic. Not angry. Just precise.

I learned who shows up when there's nothing to gain.
I learned who confuses proximity with care.
Who confuses my crisis with their opportunity.
Who confuses performance with presence.
I learned that there are levels to performance.
Imagine flying across the country only to make the catalyst for your trip feel like a layover.
Five days in town. Less than five hours with me.
A handshake where a chair should have been pulled up.
A story he probably told his wife about devotion.
About sacrifice. About how he "showed up for me."
While I lay back learning how lonely truth can be.
He didn't come to sit. He came to escape.
My pain was his alibi.
I forgive you, but I release you.

And then there were the spaces that shared my words but not my weight.
Environments that spoke in the language of care but operated in the rhythm of convenience.
Where values were articulated with fluency, but not practiced with consistency.
Where support was often offered in sentiment, but less often in function.
Where rest was encouraged, but rarely protected.
Silence dressed up as "I didn't want to bother you."

Distance justified as “I figured you had support.”
Absence explained away with good intentions that never turned into actions.

I saw the tension between what was said and what was sustained.
Learned that proximity does not guarantee participation.
That shared names do not always mean shared responsibility.
That sometimes the table is full, but no one is actually breaking bread with you.
I began to understand.
Not with bitterness, but with grace.
That not every space is designed to hold you at your depth.
That some rooms are only familiar because you learned how to shrink inside them.
And then, in the aftermath, questions about my tone.
Critiques of my boundaries.
Accusations about my distance.
They said I changed.
As if almost dying doesn’t rearrange priorities.
As if acting on clarity is a crime.

Because somewhere between the IV drip and the quiet hours when night nurses whisper prayers without words...
I realized something holy.
It didn’t matter that none of them had me.
God did.
Instead of breaking me, that truth set me free.

Because when you stop expecting nourishment from empty cups, you stop starving.
I stopped overexplaining.
Stopped overextending.
Stopped bleeding into rooms that wouldn’t even hand me a towel.
I stopped confusing history with obligation.
Stopped calling access “love.”
Stopped calling endurance “relationship.”
Forgiveness, I learned, is not always reconciliation.
Sometimes forgiveness is releasing the hope that someone will become who they’ve already showed you they are not.

So, I forgive you.
For what you could not give.
For what you would not give.
For what you pretended to give.
And I release you.
From my expectations.
From my energy.
From the sacred space where my healing now lives.
This is not bitterness.
This is boundaries with a heartbeat.

I am no longer available for relationships that drain my battery and don't fill my cup.
For those who take but never give, yet still call it connection.
I am no longer investing in people who benefit from my depletion.
I don't need revenge.
I don't need closure conversations.
I don't need apologies that arrive late and leave early.
I have peace. And peace is expensive real estate.

So, take this gently, but take it clearly:
You are forgiven.
You are released.
I bless you on your way out.
I thank you for the lesson.
And I finally make room for the relationships that know the difference between being around and being there.
God is curating a village for me.
A village of abundance and connection.
And unfortunately, you don't meet the minimum qualifications.

NOTICING & INTEGRATION

CLARITY & TRUTH

Healing often begins with honesty. Not the kind of honesty that blames or attacks, but the kind that allows us to acknowledge what is actually true.

- Who in your life has not shown up for you in the way you needed?
- What specifically did they do or fail to do?
- What impact did that have on you emotionally, mentally, physically, or spiritually?
- On a scale of 1–10, how willing are you to see this relationship clearly, without minimizing, justifying, or rewriting reality?
- What would you see differently if you were one point higher?

PATTERNS & REALIZATIONS

Sometimes we continue carrying relationships long after they stop carrying us. History can feel like obligation. Hope can sometimes keep us attached to a version of someone that only exists in our imagination.

- Have you confused history with obligation in any of your relationships?
- Where have you continued giving access to people who consistently depleted, disappointed, or diminished you?
- What have you tolerated that you would never advise someone you love to tolerate?
- On a scale of 1–10, how clearly do you understand what is and is not acceptable in your relationships today?
- What would be different if you were one point higher?

FORGIVENESS & RELEASE

Forgiveness and reconciliation are not the same thing. Sometimes peace comes not from repairing the relationship, but from releasing the expectation that it will become something it may be unable to be.

- What would it mean to forgive someone without restoring the relationship?
- What expectations are you ready to release?
- What boundaries are now necessary to protect your peace, energy, and well-being?
- On a scale of 1–10, how free do you feel to choose peace over guilt when making relationship decisions?
- If that number moved one point higher, what would become easier to release?

WHAT'S ALREADY TRUE

You likely know much more than you think you do. The truth has often been present long before acceptance arrives. Many of us stay stuck not because we lack information, but because we are still hoping the information will change.

- What are you already doing that suggests you are beginning to choose yourself more?
- When have you already seen someone's behavior clearly show you who they were?
- What becomes possible when you trust that you do not need more evidence in order to make a healthy decision?

MICRO PRACTICE
THE RELEASE STATEMENT

Release does not require anger. It does not require revenge. It does not require a dramatic confrontation. Sometimes release begins with telling the truth. This practice is about accepting reality as it is.

Find a quiet space. Take a few slow breaths.

NAME REALITY

Complete this sentence:

"I accept that ____ is not able or willing to show up for me in the way I need."

Do not soften it.
Do not explain it away.
Do not argue with it.
Simply tell the truth.

RELEASE THE EXPECTATION

Write this sentence exactly:

"I release the expectation that they will become who I needed them to be."

Pause. Read it again.
Notice what emotions surface.

CHOOSE YOURSELF

Complete the following:

"The peace I have been waiting for requires ____."
"Moving forward, I will protect my peace by ____."
"What I need most in this season is ____."

Be specific.
Focus on actions, not intentions.

ANCHOR THE DECISION

Write this sentence exactly:

"This is not about punishment. This is about alignment."

Then sign your name beneath it.
Not as a contract with them.
As a commitment to yourself.

CARRY THIS FORWARD

You do not need revenge.

You do not need the perfect apology. You do not need the closure conversation that finally makes everything make sense. You do not need someone else's understanding before you are allowed to heal. What you need is peace.

Peace often begins where bargaining ends.
The moment you stop negotiating with reality. The moment you stop asking people to become who they have repeatedly shown you they are not prepared to be. The moment you stop carrying responsibility for choices that were never yours to make.

This does not mean becoming bitter. It does not mean becoming cold. It does not mean pretending you never cared. In fact, some of the most loving decisions you will ever make involve distance. Some of the healthiest boundaries you will ever establish will be with people you still love.

Because love and access are not the same thing. Compassion and proximity are not the same thing. Forgiveness and reconciliation are not the same thing. You can love someone. You can forgive someone. You can pray for someone. And still decide they no longer have access to your peace.

That is not cruelty. That is wisdom. That is not rejection. That is discernment. That is not bitterness. That is self-respect with boundaries. And sometimes, that is exactly what healing requires.

THINGS I LOST IN THE FIRE

There is a difference between releasing a person and releasing a life.

A person can be part of the story. A life can become the story. The plans you made. The future you imagined. The version of yourself you expected to become. The timeline you thought would unfold. The certainty you built your hopes around.

Sometimes when we let go, we aren't simply grieving what happened. We're grieving what we believed would happen. The marriage that never became what it promised. The career that stopped fitting. The friendship that couldn't survive growth. The opportunity that looked permanent until it wasn't. The future that quietly dissolved while you were still making plans for it.

And perhaps that is why some transitions feel less like change and more like loss. Because they are. There is no healing without honesty. And honesty requires us to acknowledge that some endings hurt precisely because they mattered. Not everything we release was toxic. Not everything we release was terrible. Not everything we release was easy to walk away from. Sometimes we are letting go of things we genuinely loved. Things that shaped us. Things that carried us through important seasons. Things that helped us become who we are.

The challenge is that gratitude and release can coexist. You can appreciate what something gave you and still recognize that it can no longer go where you're headed. You can honor a season without remaining trapped inside it. You can thank something for its service without renewing its lease on your future.

But before that freedom arrives, there is often a fire. A season where certainty burns. Where old structures collapse. Where the things you thought would save you fail to survive the heat. In that fire, something remarkable happens. You discover what was temporary. You discover what was true.

The next piece is not about destruction. It is about revelation. About what remains when the smoke clears. About what becomes possible when you're finally willing to lose what no longer aligns with who you're becoming.

THINGS I LOST IN THE FIRE

I didn't leave because it was easy.
I left because staying was teaching my spirit how to shrink.

People like to romanticize departure.
As if walking away is some clean, cinematic exit with a soundtrack swelling at the door.
But leaving is usually quiet.
Leaving sounds like cardboard tearing, keys set down where they don't belong, a last look at a room that thought it owned you.

I didn't pack everything.
I couldn't.
Some things don't fit in boxes.
Some things only leave as ash.
I lost furniture I paid for with overtime and optimism.
Lost books that had memorized my hands.
Lost routines that pretended to be safety.
Lost the version of me that kept making excuses for rooms that never warmed.
I lost certainty.
I lost comfort that came with conditions.
I lost a future that required me to be smaller than my calling.

And yes...
I lost things that still mattered to me.
That's the part people skip.
They talk about toxic relationships like they're easy villains, but even the wrong house can feel like home when you've lived inside it long enough.
There were moments I stood in the doorway counting what I was about to give up.
The house.
The savings.
There were moments my hands shook because survival was asking me to trust God without collateral.

Walking away felt like lighting a match to everything I'd built with good intentions and misdirected loyalty.
It felt irresponsible.

It felt reckless.
It felt like faith without a safety net.
But here's what I learned about fire...
It doesn't just destroy.
It reveals.
It showed me what was flammable and what was forged.
It burned away the clutter I mistook for stability.
It took the weight so I could feel my feet again.
I had to be willing to lose everything I had if I wanted to gain everything I was meant for.

That's the line nobody wants to say out loud.
Because we prefer upgrades to surrender.
Additions to excavation.
We want blessings stacked on top of the same structures that were already cracking our foundations.
But God doesn't renovate what needs to be released.

I had to stop believing that I could carry my future without setting down my past.
Had to accept that what I wanted couldn't coexist with what I was tolerating.
Leaving wasn't bravery.
It was obedience with trembling hands.
I walked away with less stuff and more peace.
More silence.
More room for breath to move freely again.
More room for God to speak without competing with chaos I kept calling familiar.

Some days I miss what burned.
That doesn't mean the fire was wrong.
It means I'm human.
But I don't miss the version of me who kept negotiating with pain.
I don't miss the way my joy had to ask permission.
I don't miss waking up already tired from carrying burdens that weren't mine to bear.

What I gained doesn't fit in a storage unit.
I gained alignment.

I gained peace that doesn't require explanation.
I gained the kind of clarity that only comes after everything nonessential is gone.
I learned that loss can be holy.
That shedding is not failure.
That sometimes strength is stepping into the unknown with empty hands and a full trust.

So, if you're standing in your own doorway right now, counting what you might lose, hear me clearly.
You are not wrong for hesitating.
You are not weak for grieving what you're leaving.
But you are allowed to choose the life you were built for even if it costs you the life you built.
Because what God has for you will not require you to stay where you are shrinking.
In fact, it won't allow you to.

What waits on the other side of the fire is not absence.
It's becoming.

NOTICING & INTEGRATION

COUNTING THE COST

Every meaningful transition costs something. Time. Comfort. Predictability. Identity. Sometimes we know exactly what we are leaving. Other times we only discover the cost once we begin walking away.

- What are you currently afraid you might lose if you fully honor what you know is true?
- What have you been holding onto primarily because you have already invested so much into it?
- What would be possible if fear of loss didn't shape your decisions?
- On a scale of 1–10, how willing are you to release something that no longer serves you, even if you still care about it?
- What helps make that number as high as it already is?

FAMILIARITY VS. ALIGNMENT

Our nervous systems often prefer predictable discomfort over unfamiliar freedom. We can become loyal to environments, relationships, roles, and identities long after they have stopped serving our growth.

- Where in your life have you mistaken familiarity for alignment?
- What have you been tolerating that no longer reflects who you are?
- What version of your future cannot coexist with what you are currently holding onto?
- On a scale of 1–10, how aligned does your current life feel with the future you hope to create?
- If that number moved one point higher, what would change?

FIRE & REFINEMENT

Most of us think of fire as destruction. But fire also reveals. It shows us what burns easily and what remains. It strips away what cannot survive the heat and leaves behind what is genuine, durable, and true.

- What difficult season revealed something important about you?
- What strengths, values, or truths were birthed in a fire you once thought might destroy you?
- What part of your life feels like it is currently being refined rather than ruined?
- On a scale of 1–10, how much do you trust that loss can sometimes create space for something better?
- What evidence already exists in your life that supports that belief?

WHAT'S ALREADY TRUE

You have already survived losses you once believed would define you. You have already released things that felt permanent. You have already discovered that life continues after endings. More than that, you have likely discovered that some of your greatest growth emerged from things you never would have chosen.

- When have you already experienced a painful ending that ultimately created room for something healthier, more aligned, or more meaningful?
- What strengths have emerged in your life because something did not work out the way you originally hoped?
- What would shift if you trusted that releasing something is not always losing it, but sometimes making room for what comes next?

MICRO PRACTICE
THE FIRE INVENTORY

Think about one thing you are struggling to release.

A relationship.
A role.
A belief.
A dream.
A version of yourself.
A chapter that has already ended, but that part of you is still trying to preserve.

Write it at the top of the page, then complete the following:

WHAT I AM HOLDING

The thing I am struggling to release is ____.
What I am afraid of losing is ____.
What I hope holding onto it will give me is ____.

WHAT IT IS COSTING ME

Keeping this has cost me ____.
The version of me that remains attached is trying to protect ____.
The future it may be preventing is ____.

WHAT THE FIRE REVEALED

This experience taught me ____.
What survived the fire was ____.
What I now know about myself is ____.

THE RELEASE

Write this exactly:

"I honor what this season gave me, and I release what it can no longer carry."

Then sit quietly for a moment.
Notice what emotions arise.
Grief. Relief. Resistance. Hope.
Allow them all.
Because release is rarely emotionless.
It is often the place where grief and freedom shake hands.

CARRY THIS FORWARD

There are seasons when growth looks like gain. New opportunities. New relationships. New clarity. New beginnings.

Then there are seasons when growth looks like loss. Not because life is punishing you. Because life is making room. Making room for a version of you that cannot emerge while carrying everything that came before.

That does not mean the loss is easy. It does not mean the grief is smooth. It does not mean you should pretend the ending did not matter. Some things are worth mourning. Some chapters deserve tears. Some departures deserve acknowledgment.

The goal is not to stop caring. The goal is to stop confusing caring with clinging. Because there comes a moment when what once protected you begins limiting you. A moment when what once served you begins shrinking you. A moment when obedience asks you to trust what is ahead more than what is familiar.

That moment is rarely comfortable. But it is often sacred. So, if you find yourself standing in a doorway, counting what you might lose, know this: You are allowed to grieve. You are allowed to hesitate. You are allowed to feel the weight of the decision.

But you are also allowed to choose the life you were built for. Even if it costs you the life you built. Because what waits on the other side of the fire is not emptiness. It is space. It is freedom. It is alignment. It is becoming. And sometimes becoming requires letting the fire do its work.

THE OTHER SIDE

One of the hardest parts about healing is that eventually it asks you to do more than let go. Eventually, it asks you to receive.

At first, that sounds easy. Until you realize how much loss has shaped the way you experience love. How many disappointments taught you to brace. How many betrayals taught you to question. How many endings taught you to prepare for departure before connection even had a chance to settle in.

Because pain has a way of becoming predictive. It convinces us that what happened before will happen again. That peace is temporary. That consistency is suspicious. That stability must be hiding a catch. And so, we become experts at surviving love. Analyzing it. Testing it. Questioning it. Preparing for its collapse.

But healing creates a new challenge. What happens when the thing you've been praying for finally arrives? What happens when love no longer feels chaotic? When connection no longer requires self-abandonment? When someone shows up consistently instead of occasionally? What happens when your nervous system encounters something healthy after years of adapting to what was not?

For many people, that moment is surprisingly uncomfortable. Not because healthy love is difficult. Because it is unfamiliar. And unfamiliarity has a way of masquerading as danger. Especially when chaos once felt like home.

The truth is that healing doesn't just change who you choose. It changes what you're willing to receive. Because there comes a point when the question is no longer: *"Can I survive heartbreak?"* The questions become: *"Can I trust peace?" "Can I stop interrogating what is healthy?" "Can I stop preparing for abandonment?" "Can I stop treating stability like a problem that needs solving?"*

The next piece lives on the other side of that question. On the other side of survival. On the other side of scarcity. On the other side of believing you must earn what is already trying to love you well.

ON THE OTHER SIDE

I was waiting too.
Just not the way you imagine waiting.
Not with folded hands or a neat list of hopes.
Not staring at the door asking God when.
I was becoming.
I was unlearning stories of survival that taught me to brace instead of receive.
I was setting down armor I didn't know I was allowed to take off.
I was asking God to quiet the parts of me that confused chaos for chemistry.
Consistency for boredom.
I was learning patience.
Learning discernment.
Learning how to trust my peace when it finally arrived.
Learning what I need to learn to recognize rest when it showed up.

I needed you to arrive without needing me to save you.
You needed me to arrive without needing to be earned.
So, God let us wander.
Not to punish us.
But to prepare our nervous systems for something quiet and real.
I had to learn how to stop performing strength.
How to stop proving worth.
I had to learn I deserved softness without apologizing for it.
That love didn't require self-erasure or exhaustion.

You waited on the Lord while he worked on me.
You prayed for a man who knew how to listen.
Not just to words, but to silence.
A man who could sit in a room without trying to fix it.
Who knew the difference between presence and pressure.
And every time you were delayed.
Every time you thought you missed your moment.
God smiled.
Because he was working on you too.
Preparing you to hold joy without interrogating it.
Preparing you to rest without asking what comes next.
Preparing you to lean in without fear of losing yourself.

I'd go through it all again if I knew this was waiting on the other side.
I'd go through it twice.
Every ache. Every long night.
Every unanswered prayer that was actually God saying...
"Not yet. You're still learning how to hold space for her, and she is still learning to occupy it."

When we finally crossed paths, it was fireworks.
It was exhale. It was recognition.
You didn't feel claimed. You felt covered.
I didn't feel needed. I felt necessary.
That's how I knew.
Not because my heart raced, though it did.
Not because my body rested, though it did.
Because my spirit didn't need armor.
Because my joy didn't feel borrowed.

If you ever wonder, as I often have, why we didn't meet sooner.
Look at how easily we breathe together.
Look at how peace didn't need instructions.
Look at how God didn't rush us once He finally introduced us.
This is what the waiting was for.
Not just love, but alignment.
Not just partnership, but permission.
To be our full selves without negotiation.
You waited on the Lord. I did too.
And He did not waste a single moment.
Not on your side. Not on mine. Not on ours.

NOTICING & INTEGRATION

OLD PATTERNS

Love teaches us. Sometimes beautifully. Sometimes painfully. And sometimes the way we learned love in one season becomes the very pattern we have to unlearn in another.

- What has love looked like for you in the past?
- Where have you confused intensity or urgency with real connection?
- Where have you felt responsible for fixing, or saving someone?
- On a scale of 1–10, how clearly can you recognize the difference between love that feels familiar and love that is healthy?
- If you were one point higher, what would be different?

READINESS

Healthy love often requires a different version of us. A more honest one. A version willing to receive without performing, communicate without collapsing, and set boundaries without apology.

- In what ways have you grown into someone who can now receive healthier relationships?
- What have you had to unlearn about love or worthiness?
- What boundaries have you developed that support healthier connection?
- On a scale of 1–10, how ready do you feel to receive healthy, stable love?
- How would you approach connection differently if you were one point higher?

RECEIVING WITHOUT FEAR

Peace can feel suspicious when chaos has been familiar. When your nervous system is used to bracing, stability may feel like something to investigate instead of something to enjoy.

- What feels unfamiliar, but good, in your relationships right now?
- Where do you find yourself questioning or overanalyzing something that is stable?
- What would it look like to trust peace instead of interrogating it?
- On a scale of 1–10, how much do you trust yourself not to sabotage something good?
- If that number moved one point higher, what would you allow yourself to experience more fully?

WHAT'S ALREADY TRUE

You are not starting from scratch. You have already learned things about love, connection, boundaries, and your own needs that an earlier version of you did not know. Your capacity to receive is already be growing in quiet, ordinary ways.

- How are you already showing up in relationships in ways an earlier version of you could not?
- When have you already experienced peace in connection, even briefly? What made that possible, and what helped you stay present for it?
- What changes when you stop treating worthiness like something you must prove before you are allowed to receive love, care, or consistency?

MICRO PRACTICE

DON'T INTERRUPT THE GOOD

Some of us have become highly skilled at noticing what could go wrong. We scan. We question. We brace. We rehearse disappointment before it arrives because some part of us believes preparation will soften the blow. But constantly preparing for loss can keep us from fully receiving what is present. This is about practice noticing what feels good without immediately interrogating it.

For the next 24 hours, when something feels peaceful, supportive, consistent, joyful, gentle, or safe, pause...

Do not rush to explain it.
Do not minimize it.
Do not search for the catch.
Do not ask how long it will last.

Simply notice it, then say to yourself:

"This is safe enough for this moment."

"I can receive this."

"I do not have to earn what is already being offered with care."

If you are in a relationship, friendship, family connection, or community space where something good is happening, allow yourself to stay present for it.
If someone shows kindness, receive it.
If someone offers consistency, notice it.
If something feels peaceful, let it be peaceful before you make it complicated.

At the end of the day, write down three moments you did not interrupt.

They do not need to be dramatic.
A kind text. A quiet laugh. A moment of ease.
A conversation where your body did not brace.
A small example of care.
Let those moments become evidence.
Not proof that nothing will ever hurt again.
Evidence that your life is capable of holding something softer than survival.

CARRY THIS FORWARD

You do not have to chase what is aligned.

You do not have to prove yourself to what is meant to meet you with care. You do not have to exhaust yourself trying to hold something that is designed to hold you too.

Healthy love will still require effort. It will require honesty. Communication. Repair. Patience. Growth. But it should not require self-abandonment. It should not demand that you shrink to stay connected. It should not ask you to earn your place every morning and audition for security every night.

Sometimes the deepest shift is not finding better love. Sometimes it is becoming less suspicious of peace. Less addicted to intensity. Less invested in struggle as proof of depth.

Sometimes the work is allowing yourself to receive what no longer requires you to perform. To let steadiness be enough. To let consistency count. To let your body learn a new language.

Because when something is aligned, your spirit may recognize it before your fear knows what to do with it. Your mind may still question. Your body may still brace. Your old patterns may still whisper that calm is too quiet to be trusted.

But healing invites you to pause before you run. To notice before you sabotage. To receive before you interrogate. You did not arrive here by accident. You became someone who could stand closer to peace without needing to turn it into chaos.

So let the good be good. Let love be gentle. Let connection be steady. And let yourself believe, even if only one breath at a time, that you are allowed to be held without having to disappear.

I PRAY FOR YOU

Receiving healthy love changes you.

Not because it solves everything. Not because it removes every insecurity. Not because it suddenly erases every scar. But because it introduces a new possibility. A different way of relating. A different way of loving. A different way of being loved.

And once you've experienced that shift, something else begins to happen. You start examining the way you love other people. The expectations you carry. The fears you project. The outcomes you try to control. The burdens you accidentally place on the people you care about.

Because many of us learned that love meant responsibility. And responsibility slowly became management. Management slowly became control. And control disguised itself as concern.

We called it helping. We called it protecting. We called it wanting the best for someone. But underneath it all was often a quieter truth: We were struggling to trust their journey. Struggling to trust their timing. Struggling to trust that people can grow without us orchestrating every step.

The challenge is that love was never meant to be ownership. It was never meant to be management. It was never meant to be the slow reshaping of another human being into a version that feels safer for us.

Real love does something far more courageous. It sees clearly. It honors freely. It encourages intentionally. It releases control. Because the highest form of love is not changing someone. It is believing in them. It is creating space for them to become. It is standing beside them without standing in their way.

The next piece is about that kind of love. The kind that doesn't need to possess. The kind that doesn't need to control. The kind that trusts enough to pray. And then let God do what only God can do.

I PRAY FOR YOU

I pray for you.
Not out of fear.
Not because you lack.
Not because something is wrong.
I pray for you because gratitude needs a language, and prayer is the only one that knows how to hold it adequately.
I thank God for you exactly as you are.
For the way your presence steadies rooms.
For the way your laughter resets my nervous system.
For the way you love without spectacle.
Care without condition.
Move with intention even when no one is watching.

I don't pray for you to become someone else.
I pray that nothing dims what already shines.
That your tenderness stays protected.
That your confidence stays rooted.
That your kindness never convinces you to shrink yourself for smaller imaginations.
I pray for your dreams.
The ones you speak out loud and the ones you hold quietly like heirlooms.
I pray they arrive without requiring you to abandon yourself.
That doors open without you knocking until your knuckles forget joy.
That provision meets you early, not after exhaustion.
That celebration finds you before you've had a chance to brace for disappointment.

I pray for your peace.
Not the kind that avoids conflict.
The kind that survives truth.
The kind that lets you rest without guilt.
Say "no" without explanation.
Say "yes" without fear.
I pray that your body feels safe moving through the world.
That your heart stays soft.
That your spirit remains curious, playful, alive.
That love never feels like labor to you.

And yes, I pray for us.
Not from anxiety.
From reverence.
I ask God to keep us aligned.
To help us choose each other with clarity, not obligation.
To teach us how to love in ways that honor Him and honor who we are becoming.
I pray that we bless one another.
That we sharpen without cutting.
That we grow without outgrowing the grace between us.
That we remain gentle with each other's wounds and brave with each other's futures.
I pray that when we stumble, we learn.
When we succeed, we stay humble.
When the world gets loud, we remember why we chose each other in the first place.
I pray that love never becomes routine.
That gratitude never becomes assumed.
That we never forget how sacred it is to be trusted with someone's heart.

I don't pray for you because I need God to fix anything.
I pray because I recognize the blessing that you are.
I pray because God deserves to be exalted for his masterpiece.

When I say I pray for you, what I really mean is... I love you.

NOTICING & INTEGRATION

LOVE & CONTROL

Love often begins with good intentions. We want people to succeed. We want them to avoid pain. But sometimes what begins as care can quietly become management or correction.

- When have your efforts to "help" shown up as control?
- What fears drive your desire to fix, guide, or influence others?
- What would it look like to simply trust someone's process?
- On a scale of 1–10, how comfortable are you allowing people to make their own choices, even when you would choose differently?
- What would you do differently if that number were one point higher?

HONORING VS. IMPROVING

One of the greatest gifts we can offer another person is the experience of being fully seen without immediately being evaluated. Many relationships become improvement projects.

- Who in your life do you genuinely appreciate as they are?
- How often do you express that appreciation without attaching expectations, advice, or correction?
- Where might you be unintentionally asking someone to shrink, change, or perform in order to earn your comfort?
- On a scale of 1–10, how intentional are you about expressing appreciation and gratitude in your relationships?
- What would be different if you were one point higher on that scale?

LOVE AS STEWARDSHIP

Love is not ownership. It is stewardship. To steward someone well is not to direct their life. It is to care for the space between you in a way that allows both people to grow.

- What does it mean to "hold" someone well?
- How do you want people to feel in your presence?
- What would it look like to love someone in a way that strengthens rather than burdens them?
- On a scale of 1–10, how aligned are your actions with the kind of love you want to offer?
- If that number moved one point higher, what would you say more often, do more consistently, or stop trying to control?

WHAT'S ALREADY TRUE

You already know something about healthy love. You have likely experienced moments where connection felt safe, honoring, spacious, and genuine. You may already be practicing forms of love that create freedom instead of pressure.

- What are you already doing that suggests you are learning to love in healthier, more intentional ways?
- When have you experienced love that felt safe, honoring, and non-controlling? What made that experience possible?
- What changes when you trust that love is not something you must manage, but something you get to cultivate?

MICRO PRACTICE

SPEAK LIFE WITHOUT AN AGENDA

Many of us communicate with a hidden objective. We want improvement. Change. Correction. Movement. Results. This practice invites something different.

For the next 24 hours...

Choose one person you care about. Someone who matters to you.

Then intentionally tell them something that:

- Affirms who they are
- Expresses gratitude
- Acknowledges their impact
- Recognizes a strength you admire

Don't include advice, correction, suggestion, or expectation.
Simply offer the gift. For example:
"I appreciate the way you show up for people."
"I admire your resilience."
"I'm grateful for the impact you've had on my life."
"I want you to know that I see how hard you've been working."

Then stop.
Let the affirmation stand on its own.
Do not explain it.
Do not qualify it.
Do not follow it with "but."

Afterward, reflect:

How did it feel to encourage without directing?
How did it feel to appreciate without improving?
What did you notice in yourself?
What did you notice in them?

Sometimes the most powerful form of love is not helping someone become more. It is helping them remember that who they already are matters.

CARRY THIS FORWARD

Love is not proven through intensity.

It is revealed through consistency. Through presence. Through attention. Through the willingness to honor another person's humanity without trying to redesign it.

You do not need to fix people to love them. You do not need to rescue them to care about them. You do not need to manage their growth to support it.

The people you love are not projects. They are people. People with their own timing. Their own lessons. Their own conversations with God. Their own becoming.

One of the greatest acts of trust is believing that someone can grow without your constant intervention. Not because you do not care. Because you do. Deeply. Enough to allow them ownership of their own journey.

The highest form of love is not: "I need you to become something for me." It is: "I am grateful for who you already are." That kind of love creates room. Room to breathe. Room to grow. Room to fail. Room to heal. Room to become.

When love moves like that, it does not restrict. It expands. It becomes less about control and more about blessing. Less about management and more about presence. Less about changing people and more about honoring them.

May your love leave people stronger than it found them. And may you learn to offer that same grace to yourself.

AS FOR ME AND MY HOUSE

Loving well changes the way you relate to people.

But eventually, it also changes the way you relate to yourself. Because every healthy relationship teaches the same lesson: What you allow shapes what you experience. What you tolerate shapes what grows. What you protect shapes what survives.

Whether we realize it or not, we are all building something. A life. A family. A culture. A reputation. A set of habits. A collection of daily decisions that eventually become the architecture of our future.

The challenge is that most people inherit that architecture. They inherit beliefs. Priorities. Patterns. Expectations. Definitions of success. Definitions of love. Definitions of worth. And then spend years living inside structures they never consciously chose. Until one day they pause long enough to ask: *Do I actually want to build my life this way?*

Because there comes a moment in every growth journey when healing is no longer the primary task. The task becomes alignment. Not discovering what matters. Living like it matters. Not identifying your values. Protecting them. Not admiring the life you want. Building it. Brick by brick. Choice by choice. Boundary by boundary.

The beautiful thing about clarity is that it simplifies decisions. Once you know what you're building, some things become easier to release. Some invitations become easier to decline. Some compromises become impossible to justify. Not because you're rigid. Because you're rooted.

The next piece is a declaration. A line in the sand. A decision about what gets access to your life and what does not. Because eventually, every person must answer a question: *What will this life be built upon?*

AS FOR ME AND MY HOUSE

I've come to learn that faith isn't volume.
It doesn't need a microphone.
It doesn't flex, it bows.
Because the moment I start thinking I'm large, God reminds me how small the door is that purpose walks through.
I used to think calling meant confidence.
Now I know it means consent.
It means waking up and saying, "Thank you for ordering my steps; even the ones I don't understand yet."
Especially those.

Because ego will tell you that you're *chosen* when what God really said was *available*.
Pride will convince you you're *powerful* when you were only *positioned*.
I am not self-made. I am sustained.
Every breath I've taken was loaned.
Every door that opened already had my name written on the hinge before I learned how to knock.
I've learned that the most dangerous prayer is the one where you ask God to bless what He never assigned.
So, I stopped asking Him to cosign my plans and started asking Him to help me discern His.

Because obedience is not passive.
It's disciplined surrender.
It's choosing alignment over applause.
It's trusting that the path you didn't pick still leads exactly where you're supposed to arrive.
I've had moments where my talent tried to outrun my character.
Where my mouth spoke before my spirit listened.
Where I confused momentum with mandate.
And God...
Patient as ever, slowed me down with mercy.

Because being called to something higher doesn't mean being lifted above others.
It means being rooted deeper.
It means knowing I don't set the tempo.

I follow the beat God has already produced and pray that I don't show up like I have two left feet.
My steps are ordered.
Not optimized.
Not rushed.
Ordered.
Which means delay is not denial.
Silence is not absence.
And detours are often the clearest proof that God is still directing traffic.

As for me, I refuse to build a house where God is a guest.
A decoration.
A weekend visitor.
A verse I pull out when things fall apart.
He is the foundation.
The frame.
The fire in the hearth.
The reason the doors stay open and the reason some stay closed.
Because covering matters.
What you invite in matters.
What you entertain eventually moves in.

So, my house is guarded by prayer.
Furnished with humility.
Insured by grace.
We don't worship success here.
We don't chase influence.
We don't confuse provision with permission.
We serve God.
Even when the numbers don't add up.
Even when the crowd thins out.
Even when obedience costs more than disobedience ever did.
Especially then.

Because surrender isn't weakness, it's accuracy.
It's knowing my strength works best when it knows where it came from.
I don't need to be the source, and I'm fooling myself if I think I am.
What I need is to stay connected.
So, I will keep choosing reverence over relevance.
Calling over comfort.

Alignment over ambition.
Transition over temptation.

When my name is spoken.
When my work is remembered.
When my life is weighed.
Let it be said that I didn't center myself in what God entrusted me to steward.
Let it be said that I knew His voice.
That my steps honored His order.
That my surrender stayed intact even when my hands were full.
As for me and my house, we will serve the Lord.

NOTICING & INTEGRATION

VALUES & FOUNDATION

Every life is built on something. Sometimes we build intentionally. Sometimes the life we are living was constructed around urgency, approval, fear, survival, or someone else's expectations.

- What do you want your life to be built on at its core?
- What values are non-negotiable for you moving forward?
- What have you learned about what truly matters?
- On a scale of 1–10, how clearly can you name the values you want guiding your life?
- What would be different if you were one point higher?

ALIGNMENT & INTEGRITY

Integrity is not only about what we believe. It is about whether our choices reflect what we believe when life becomes inconvenient. Alignment asks us to close the gap between conviction and behavior.

- Where in your life are you currently misaligned with your values?
- What would change if you fully honored what you say you believe?
- What does integrity look like for you on a daily basis?
- On a scale of 1–10, how aligned is your current life with your core values?
- If that number moved one point higher, what decision would become clearer or easier to make?

ENVIRONMENT & INFLUENCE

Your "house" is more than where you live. It is what you allow into your mind, your relationships, your routines, your attention, your spirit. What you allow repeatedly becomes part of what shapes you.

- What are you allowing into your "house" mentally, emotionally, spiritually, or relationally?
- What needs to be removed, limited, protected, or more carefully tended?
- What do you want your environment to reinforce about who you are becoming?
- On a scale of 1–10, how consistently are you living according to what you say matters most?
- If that number moved one point higher, what habit would you reinforce or what boundary would you hold more firmly?

WHAT'S ALREADY TRUE

You are already building something. Every choice, habit, boundary, relationship, and repeated practice is shaping the house of your life. You may already have more evidence of alignment than you realize.

- What are you already doing that suggests you are building a life that reflects who you truly are?
- When have you already experienced alignment between your values and your actions?
- What changes when you trust that you are capable of living in alignment not just occasionally, but consistently?

MICRO PRACTICE
DEFINE YOUR STANDARD

A standard is different from a wish. A wish hopes life will change. A standard names what you are willing to live by. This practice is not about creating a perfect version of yourself. It is about clarifying the life you are choosing to build.

Complete the following:

Take your time. Write slowly.
Let each sentence become instruction.

IDENTITY

"As for me, I am someone who ____."

"At my core, I am someone who ____."

Read both aloud. Notice whether they sound like truth or performance.

VALUES

"My life is built on ____."

"The values that guide my decisions are ____."

Be specific. Name values that can actually shape behavior.

BOUNDARIES

"I no longer allow ____."

"What no longer has access to my peace is ____."

This is where alignment becomes protection.

COMMITMENT

"Moving forward, I commit to ____."

"The version of me I am choosing to practice daily will ____."

Make this practical. Something visible. Something measurable.

ALIGNMENT

"Even when it is difficult, I will choose ____."

"When fear, doubt, or discomfort arise, I will remain aligned with ____."

This is the declaration.
Not because it will always be easy. Because it matters.
Return to these statements often.
They are not decorative. They are directional.

CARRY THIS FORWARD

You do not need to figure out who you are anymore. Not in the way you once did. You have done enough searching to know what matters. You have lived enough life to recognize what drains you. You have survived enough seasons to understand what cannot come with you.

Now the work is different. Now the work is living like it. Not occasionally. Not when it is convenient. Not when everyone understands. Not when the conditions are perfect. Consistently.

Because your life will always reflect what you tolerate, what you prioritize, and what you practice. It will reflect what you protect. What you ignore. What you repeat. What you allow. What you return to. A house is not built by intention alone. It is built by decisions. Daily ones. Quiet ones. Costly ones. The kind nobody applauds, but everyone eventually sees.

So, choose carefully. Build intentionally. Protect what matters. Release what contradicts your becoming. And stand firmly in the decision that you are no longer available for a life that requires you to betray who you have become in order to keep it.

This is not about perfection. It is about alignment. And alignment is not something you visit when life gets quiet. It is something you practice until it becomes the atmosphere of your life.

As for you and your house, build accordingly.

CONVERSATIONS

There is a beautiful confidence that comes with alignment.

The confidence of knowing what matters. The confidence of knowing what you stand for. The confidence of deciding what belongs in your life and what no longer does.

But alignment does not eliminate uncertainty. In many ways, it creates new questions. Because once you've stopped blaming everyone else... Once you've stopped living according to someone else's expectations... Once you've begun building a life that actually reflects your values... You eventually encounter something unavoidable: The limits of your own understanding.

There are still seasons that don't make sense. Still losses you cannot fully explain. Still prayers that seem unanswered. Still moments when life asks questions you don't know how to answer. And perhaps that is where many people get stuck. Not because they lack faith. Because they expected faith to eliminate mystery.

But faith was never the absence of questions. Faith is often the willingness to keep asking them. To wrestle honestly. To remain curious. To sit with uncertainty long enough for wisdom to emerge. Some of the most transformative moments in life do not arrive through certainty. They arrive through conversation. The difficult conversations. The uncomfortable conversations. The conversations where we stop trying to sound wise and start telling the truth. The conversations where we stop presenting our polished answers and begin offering our honest questions. And perhaps nowhere is that more important than in our relationship with God. Because growth often begins when prayer stops being performance and becomes dialogue.

The next piece is about those moments. The moments when faith stops pretending. The moments when questions become sacred. The moments when we discover that some of our deepest growth happens not despite the conversation, but because of it.

CONVERSATIONS

Father...
Did I really have to go through all that?
Every bruise.
Every betrayal.
Every night I begged the ceiling for silence.
Was all that pain required just to reach this peace?
Wasn't there an easier way to teach me what I know now?
Couldn't I have learned some of those lessons secondhand?
Through whispers, through witness, through warning instead of wounds?

"I tried to teach you those lessons secondhand.
But you were too busy thinking you were helping other people fix their problems.
Not realizing I was presenting solutions for yours.
You prayed for revelation but ran from reflection.
So yes, it was necessary to go through every one of those storms.
Because you were too stubborn to recognize the rain when it was falling.
Too eager to claim that you were unbothered by it.
So, I had to turn it into a hurricane.
But know this, my son... I never sent a storm without a coat.
You were never unprotected.
I was always there.
Remember the riddle of the sphinx. When you crawled on four, I was there. When you grew and walked on two, I was there. And when you walk on three; I will be the third.
Because in that moment, you will need me more than ever."

I hear you.
But I won't pretend I don't still wrestle.
Not with ideas, with memories.
With moments I can still point to and say, "that right there didn't make sense."
I've watched people I love carry pain they did not earn.
Watched good hearts get tested like they owed the world something.
Watched men try to hold their families together with hands that were already shaking.
Watched women pray through things that should have never required prayer in the first place.

And I remember thinking: "where were you in that?"
Not as accusation. As confusion.
I've seen the kind of hurt that doesn't just visit, it settles in.
The kind that changes how someone laughs.
How they trust.
How they show up in rooms that used to feel like home.

And I've tried to make sense of it.
Tried to find a clean explanation for something that never felt clean.
Why does pain land on people who were already carrying too much?
Why does harm reach where it should have been blocked?
Why does darkness get access to spaces that were supposed to be covered?
I don't ask that like someone looking for a debate.
I ask that like someone who remembers faces.
Who remembers names.
Who remembers stories that didn't deserve the chapters they were given.
And if I'm honest, my faith wasn't built in clarity.
It was built in the tension of not understanding and choosing anyway.
Somewhere between what I saw and what I believe, I made a decision to trust you anyway.
Because I've also seen what happens when you step in.
I've seen restoration rewrite what seemed permanent.
I've seen people come back from places that didn't have exits.
I've seen healing take root in ground that looked too broken to grow anything.
But still, I wrestle...

"Son...
Of course you wrestle with it.
You were never meant to see the full canvas.
You're so focused on the outcome that you still can't see that the only outcome is your return to me.
Until then, everything is process.
Everything, my son...
You are here to fulfill a mission, and that mission is preparation."

Preparation for what?

"Transition.

And yes, you will make that transition before you rejoin me.
You must. It is necessary.
You think you went through a lot. And you did.
I won't take that from you.
But I only give that kind of weight to my strongest soldiers.

You saw pain, but I saw process.
You named it loss, but I was making room.
You questioned the seed because all you could see was the burial.
I saw the harvest before it ever broke the surface.
You thought you were surviving a storm.
Bracing, enduring, waiting for it to pass.
But what you didn't see was what it was unlocking in you.
What it was loosening. What it was building.
What it was preparing you to carry.
You told me you couldn't stand. I told you to crawl.
Not as a compromise, but as a reminder.
Forward is still forward even when it's low to the ground.

You asked, "why me?"
And I understood the weight in that question.
But I also needed you to understand something...
This was never about punishment. It was preparation.
Because some lessons cannot be explained.
They must be lived.
They must be walked through until the understanding settles in your bones.
So, what you called suffering, I was shaping.
What you called delay, I was developing.
And what you thought was breaking you was the very thing building you into someone who could hold what you've been asking for."

NOTICING & INTEGRATION

MEANING-MAKING

Pain rarely arrives with an explanation. The story we attach to pain can either keep us trapped inside the wound or help us begin to recognize what was formed there.

- What is a painful experience that you still struggle to understand?
- What meaning have you assigned to that experience up to this point?
- How has that meaning shaped the way you see yourself, God, others, or your future?
- On a scale of 1–10, how much peace do you currently have with the parts of your story you still do not fully understand?
- What has helped that number become as high as it already is?

REFRAMING THE NARRATIVE

Reframing does not mean pretending the pain was good. It means refusing to let pain have the only interpretation. Sometimes what felt like punishment was preparation.

- What did that season force you to learn, develop, or confront that you may not have learned otherwise?
- In what ways did you become stronger, wiser, more discerning, or more aware as a result?
- On a scale of 1–10, how much do you believe your challenges have contributed to your growth?
- What would change about your self-talk if you were on point higher?

RESPONSIBILITY & REFLECTION

There is a difference between blaming yourself and being honest with yourself. Sometimes change begins when we stop only asking why something happened and begin asking what the experience revealed.

- Where in your life have you been asking for change without fully engaging in reflection?
- What truths have you resisted because they challenged how you wanted to see yourself?
- What might become possible if you faced those truths with honesty and compassion?
- On a scale of 1–10, how willing are you to examine your story without collapsing into shame or defensiveness?
- If that number moved one point higher, what truth would become safer to face?

WHAT'S ALREADY TRUE

Your story is not finished being interpreted. The meaning you once made of your pain does not have to be the meaning you carry forever. Even now, there may already be evidence that your past is becoming something more than proof of what hurt you.

- What story are you already beginning to tell differently, even if only to yourself?
- When have you already seen evidence that your struggle produced wisdom, strength, compassion, clarity, or purpose?
- What becomes possible when you trust that your life is not only happening to you, but forming something within you?

MICRO PRACTICE
THE STORM REFRAME

Some storms do not make sense while we are standing in them. But over time, with enough distance and enough honesty, we may begin to see more than what the storm damaged. We may begin to see what it revealed, what it developed, what it forced us to confront, and what it made possible. This practice is not about minimizing your pain. It is about reclaiming authorship over the meaning of your story.

Choose one difficult experience that still carries emotional weight.

Start with something you can approach honestly without overwhelming yourself.

THE OLD NARRATIVE

Write from the meaning you have carried up to this point.

What happened? Why did it hurt? What did you lose? What did you begin believing about yourself, others, or the world because of it?

Let this version tell the truth about the pain.

Don't sanitize it. Do not rush past it. Name what was real.

THE EMERGING NARRATIVE

Now write from the perspective of the person you are becoming.

What did that experience reveal? What did it develop in you? What did it clarify?
What did it teach you about your needs, your strength, your boundaries, your calling, or your capacity to keep going?
What became possible afterward that may not have been possible before?

THE QUESTION

When both versions are written, read them slowly, then ask yourself:

"Which version gives me more power to move forward?"

That does not mean choosing the prettier version.
It means choosing the truer, fuller, more freeing version.
The old narrative may explain your pain.
But the emerging narrative can help guide your healing.
Begin practicing the version that gives you back your agency.

CARRY THIS FORWARD

You may not understand everything that happened.

You may never receive the full explanation you once believed you needed. Some questions may remain unanswered. Some losses may never feel fair. Some storms may never become something you would have chosen.

And still, your life can keep unfolding with meaning. Healing does not require you to call pain good. It does not require you to be grateful for what broke your heart. It does not require you to pretend the storm was gentle. Healing simply asks whether pain gets to be the final narrator.

Because there is a difference between what happened to you and what is still being formed in you. There is a difference between being wounded and being only your wound. There is a difference between surviving something and surrendering your entire identity to it.

So, ask your questions. Wrestle honestly. Tell God the truth. But do not stop there. Listen for what the storm revealed. Notice what it strengthened. Honor what it clarified. And when you are ready, begin telling the story in a way that does not erase the pain, but refuses to erase your power.

You were not abandoned. You were not forgotten. You were not reduced to what happened. Somewhere between your questions and God's response, something in you was being prepared. And what was prepared in the storm may still become part of what carries you forward.

NOT BY SIGHT

Some conversations change the way you think. Others change the way you live. The difference is trust.

Because eventually every question reaches a point where more analysis stops helping. Not because curiosity is bad. Not because reflection lacks value. But because there comes a moment when the next lesson cannot be learned through understanding alone. It must be experienced.

Most of us prefer clarity before movement. We want the map before the journey. The guarantee before the commitment. The outcome before the investment. We want to know exactly how things will unfold before we agree to take the first step. And honestly? That makes sense. Certainty feels safe. Predictability feels responsible. Control feels comforting.

But life rarely unfolds that way. Some of the most important decisions we ever make arrive with incomplete information. The career change. The relationship. The move. The calling. The dream. The act of obedience that makes absolutely no sense to anyone except the person who has been carrying it. And that is where faith becomes more than belief. Faith becomes movement.

Because it is one thing to pray for guidance. It is another thing entirely to follow it. One thing to ask for direction. Another to take the step when the destination remains partially hidden. The truth is, many of the things we are waiting to see can only be seen after we start walking. The path reveals itself through participation. The confidence grows through action. The evidence appears through movement. Not before it. After it. Which means there comes a point where the question is no longer: *"What do I know?"* The questions become "*What do I trust?" "Do I trust what I cannot yet measure?" "Do I trust what I cannot yet explain?" "Do I trust myself enough to move before certainty arrives?"*

The next piece lives inside those questions. Inside the uncomfortable space between knowing and seeing. Between belief and proof. Between hesitation and action. Because some journeys can only be traveled one step at a time. And some truths can't be discovered by sight.

NOT BY SIGHT

I've learned that sight is persuasive.
Convincing.
Fluent in urgency.
Sight tells you to trust what's loud.
What's immediate.
What can be measured. Mapped. Verified. Explained.
Sight asks for evidence up front.
Sight wants guarantees before it commits.
Sight believes what it can touch and dismisses what it has to wait for.

But faith. Faith moves differently.
Faith doesn't deny reality.
It just refuses to let appearances have the final word.
There were seasons when what I could see told me to stop.
When what I couldn't see kept me from starting.
Told me the math didn't math.
Told me the timeline had expired.
Told me the door was closed because it looked like a wall.
And if I had trusted my eyes alone, I would've misread the moment.
Mistaken delay for denial.
Confused silence for absence.
Assumed nothing was happening because nothing was visible yet.

But God has never been bound to what's obvious.
Some of the most important work he does quietly.
Underground. Behind the scenes.
In places sight can't perceive.
Faith doesn't mean pretending things aren't hard.
It means believing they aren't finished.
It means walking forward without the comfort of clarity.
Choosing obedience before you receive understanding.
Placing your foot down before the ground reveals itself.

I've learned that sight panics when it can't predict outcomes.
Faith listens.
Sight rushes.
Faith waits.
Sight asks, *"Does this make sense?"*

Faith asks, *"Did God say move?"*
And there's a difference.
Because sight will always favor safety over calling.
Logic over obedience.
Control over trust.
Faith, on the other hand, is willing to look foolish.
It builds before the rain.
Moves before the confirmation.
Commits before the applause.

Faith understands something sight never will.
That just because you can't see the next step that doesn't mean the staircase hasn't been laid out for you.
I've survived seasons where nothing lined up on paper.
Where the numbers didn't favor me.
Where the doors I expected to open stayed shut.
And yet, somehow, I was still being held.
Provision came disguised as timing.
Protection came disguised as disappointment.
Direction came disguised as uncertainty.
And had I trusted sight, I would've turned back right before the miracle cleared its throat.

Faith taught me that God is not likely to show me the full picture.
Sometimes obedience is the vision.
Sometimes trust is the map.
Sometimes the blessing doesn't reveal itself until you've already moved.
I don't move by sight anymore.
Because sight once told me I was behind when God was actually repositioning me.
Sight once told me I had missed it when God was still preparing it.
Sight once told me to settle when God was still setting it apart.

So now I walk slower.
Listen deeper.
Pray longer.
Trust harder.
Not because I see clearly, but because I don't have to.
Faith doesn't require proof, it requires surrender.

And I've learned that God does His best work in the spaces where I stop trying to predict Him and start trusting Him instead.

So, I move not by what looks possible.
Not by what feels safe.
Not by what others can understand.
I move because He said so.
Because peace followed the instruction.
Because alignment arrived before explanation.
I move not by sight, but by faith.
And every time I do, the ground remembers my name.

NOTICING & INTEGRATION

SIGHT & FAITH

Sight is useful but sight also has limits. If we only move when everything is visible, predictable, and guaranteed, we may spend our lives waiting for certainty that was never promised.

- Where in your life are you waiting for clarity before taking action?
- What would you do if you trusted your inner wisdom, spiritual discernment, or sense of alignment more than external evidence?
- What are you afraid will happen if you move without certainty?
- On a scale of 1–10, how willing are you to take aligned action without having all the answers?
- What has helped that number become as high as it already is?

MISINTERPRETATION

Not everything that looks closed is finished. Sometimes silence is preparation. Sometimes nothing appears to be happening because the work is happening somewhere you cannot yet see.

- Where have you mistaken delay for denial?
- Where have you assumed "nothing is happening" simply because you could not see visible progress?
- What opportunities may you have walked away from because they did not make immediate sense?
- On a scale of 1–10, how much do you trust that meaningful things can be unfolding even when they are not yet visible?
- What would shift If you were just one point higher?

TRUST & OBEDIENCE

There are moments when clarity comes after movement. Not before. Sometimes the next step teaches you more than the full plan ever could.

- When have you taken a step without full clarity and been grateful that you did?
- What did that experience teach you about trust and courage?
- What is one area right now where you feel prompted to move but have not yet taken the next step?
- On a scale of 1–10, how much do you trust your ability to figure things out as you go?
- If that number moved one point higher, what decision would you stop delaying or what step would you take this week?

WHAT'S ALREADY TRUE

You have already moved without perfect certainty before. You have already made decisions with incomplete information. You have already survived uncertainty, adapted in real time, and discovered strength after the step was taken.

- What are you already doing that suggests you do not need perfect clarity in order to move forward?
- When have you seen evidence that things were working behind the scenes, even when you could not see them yet?
- What shifts when you trust that just because you cannot see it does not mean it is not being built?

MICRO PRACTICE
MOVE WITHOUT THE MAP

There are times when planning is wisdom. And there are times when planning becomes delay wearing fancy clothes. This practice is about discerning the difference.

Choose one area where you feel stuck because of a lack of clarity.

Not the biggest decision in your life.
Not the most terrifying one.
One where uncertainty has kept you paused longer than necessary.

Write it at the top of the page, then ask:

"What is the next right step, not the full plan?"

Stay there.
Do not write the ten-step strategy.
Do not try to solve the entire season.
Do not demand guarantees from a single action.
Just identify one step.

Then, complete the following:

The area where I feel stuck is ____.

The clarity I keep waiting for is ____.

The next right step available to me is ____.

I can take this step within the next 24 – 48 hours by ____.

The support or structure that would help me follow through is ____.

Once you have written it, schedule it. Once you schedule it, follow through.

Put it on your calendar.
Send the message.
Make the call.
Open the document.
Take the walk.
Start the thing.

Not because you know everything.
Because you know enough to move once.
Momentum does not require a map.
Sometimes it only requires enough trust for the next step.

CARRY THIS FORWARD

You do not need to see the whole staircase.

You do not need to understand every outcome. You do not need every person to agree, every fear to quiet down, or every variable to line up before you begin. There is wisdom in preparation. But there is also danger in waiting so long for perfect clarity that your calling becomes a concept instead of a life.

Some doors will not look like doors until you walk toward them. Some paths will not reveal themselves until your foot is already lifted. Some instructions will only make sense after obedience has begun. This does not mean move carelessly. It means move aligned. Move prayerfully. Move honestly. Move with enough humility to learn as you go and enough courage to stop confusing uncertainty with impossibility.

Because fear often asks for information it has no intention of using. It keeps requesting more proof. More signs. More guarantees. More time.

But faith asks a better question: *What is the next faithful step?* Not the whole future. Not the entire blueprint. Just the next step.

So, when the path feels unclear, slow down enough to listen. Then move. Not because you have mastered certainty. But because you are learning trust.

The question is not whether you have enough information to control the outcome. The question is whether you have enough alignment to participate in what is unfolding. You were never meant to control the whole path. Only to walk the step in front of you.

WAIT ON THE LORD

Taking the first step requires courage. Taking the second requires commitment.

But perhaps the hardest part of any journey comes after you've already begun. After you've prayed. After you've trusted. After you've moved. After you've done the thing everyone said required faith. And then... Nothing seems to happen. At least not immediately. No dramatic breakthrough. No instant transformation. No clear evidence that your effort has been rewarded. Just the quiet tension between what you've done and what you're still waiting to see.

This is where many people become discouraged. Not because they lack faith. Because they assumed faith would accelerate the timeline. They assumed obedience would eliminate the waiting. They assumed movement would produce immediate results.

But life rarely unfolds on our preferred schedule. Seeds do not sprout the moment they are planted. Muscles do not strengthen after a single workout. Trust is not built through one courageous decision. The most meaningful transformations often spend long periods developing beneath the surface. Invisible. Uncelebrated. Unconfirmed. And yet, still growing.

The challenge is that waiting can feel passive. It can feel like stagnation. It can feel like evidence that nothing is happening. But inactivity and waiting are not the same thing. One is resignation. The other is preparation. One is surrendering your future. The other is trusting that your future is still unfolding.

Because there are seasons when faith looks like movement. And there are seasons when faith looks like remaining steady after you've already moved.

The next piece is for those seasons. The seasons when the answer hasn't arrived. The seasons when the timeline feels longer than expected. The seasons when you are tempted to mistake delay for denial. Because sometimes the most courageous thing you can do is not take another step. Sometimes the most courageous thing you can do is stay faithful while you wait.

WAIT ON THE LORD

I used to think waiting was punishment.
A lobby with no chairs.
A line that never moved.
A test I kept failing because I kept checking the clock instead of listening for instructions.
I used to confuse delay with denial.
Silence with absence.
Stillness with abandonment.
I thought if God loved me, He would hurry.
But now I know, waiting was never about time.
It was about alignment.
Because if I had arrived early, I would've mishandled the blessing.
If the door had opened sooner, I would've walked through it still bleeding.
Still bargaining.
Still trying to earn what was already meant for me.

So, God slowed the pace.
Not to frustrate me.
To form me.
He let me wander long enough to learn the difference between movement and direction.
Let me build things that didn't last so I'd recognize what would.
Let me succeed loudly and ache quietly.
Until I understood that accomplishment without anchoring drifts.

I see it now.
Every closed door was insulation.
Every "not yet" was protection.
Every detour was God saying, "trust me with what you can't see yet."
I didn't just need a breakthrough.
I needed a backbone.
Didn't just need favor.
I needed discernment.
Didn't just need love.
I needed to become someone who could hold it without flinching.

There were seasons I prayed with clenched fists.
Trying to negotiate timelines.

Trying to outwork grief.
Trying to logic my way into peace.
And God, patient as ever, let me tire myself out.
Until surrender stopped sounding like loss and started sounding like rest.
Waiting taught me how to listen without interrupting heaven.
How to sit with unanswered questions without demanding refunds from faith.
How to trust that just because I couldn't see the staircase, didn't mean the next step wasn't guaranteed.

And then, when I wasn't looking for it.
When I wasn't chasing outcomes.
When I finally stopped auditioning for blessings.
Stopped bobbing and weaving surrender.
Started living in alignment.
Love arrived.
Not rushed. Not chaotic.
Not requiring me to prove anything.
Sharde didn't show up as a rescue.
She arrived as confirmation.
As peace that didn't need convincing.
As laughter that felt like permission.
As partnership that didn't compete with my calling but complemented it like harmony.

Suddenly I understood.
If I had met her earlier, I would've recognized the beauty but not known how to protect it.
If God had introduced us sooner, I would've loved her with effort instead of ease.
So yes. I would do it all again.
Every wilderness.
Every long night.
Every season of "almost."
Every prayer that felt like it bounced off the ceiling only to land back in my chest as patience.
Because now I know what was waiting for me on the other side was worth the wait.
Not just her.

The version of me who could meet her whole.
Waiting taught me that God doesn't rush masterpieces.
He refines them.
That delay is often divine choreography.
Moving things into position that you didn't even know were connected.
I no longer beg God to speed things up.
I ask Him to help me discern.
To keep me aligned.

Because waiting on the Lord isn't passive.
It's active trust.
It's obedience without applause.
It's faith that doesn't need likes.
When I look back, I don't see lost time. I see training.
I see preparation.
I see mercy disguised as patience.
I see a God who knew exactly where He was taking me and loved me enough to make sure I arrived ready.

So, if you're waiting, good.
Wait.
Breathe.
He's not late. He's not distant.
He's not confused about your address.
He's building something that won't break you when it arrives.
Wait on the Lord.
Not because you have no choice, though you don't.
Wait on the Lord because what's coming is worth meeting with steady hands and an open heart.

NOTICING & INTEGRATION

REFRAMING WAITING

Waiting can feel like punishment when we believe movement is the only evidence of progress. But not all progress is visible. Some of the most important formation happens in seasons that look still from the outside.

- Where in your life do you feel like things are taking too long?
- What story are you telling yourself about that delay?
- How is that story impacting your mindset, energy, or behavior?
- On a scale of 1–10, how patient are you in your current season of life?
- What has helped you be even this patient so far?

READINESS & GROWTH

Sometimes what we are waiting for is also waiting for a version of us who can carry it. Desire is not the same as readiness. Wanting something deeply does not always mean we are prepared to steward it wisely.

- What might you still be developing in this season?
- What skills, habits, perspectives, or disciplines are being refined right now?
- How would you need to show up differently if what you are waiting for arrived today?
- On a scale of 1–10, how ready do you feel to sustain what you are praying, hoping, or working toward?
- What would change if you were one point higher?

TRUSTING THE PROCESS

Timing often makes more sense in hindsight. There are seasons we resent while we are living them, only to later realize they protected us, positioned us, or prepared us.

- Where have you experienced delays in the past that ultimately worked in your favor?
- What did those experiences teach you about timing, preparation, or trust?
- What would it look like to trust that something is being prepared for you, even if you cannot see it yet?
- On a scale of 1–10, how much do you trust that timing may be working in your favor?
- If that number moved one point higher, what would you stop rushing, forcing, or trying to control?

WHAT'S ALREADY TRUE

You have already survived seasons where the timing did not make sense. You have already seen things arrive later than you wanted, but better than you expected. You may already have evidence that waiting is not always absence. Sometimes it is protection, preparation, and alignment in motion.

- What would shift if you believed that timing is not punishment, but preparation?
- When have you already seen that God's timing, life's timing, or a delayed outcome worked out better than your original plan?
- What changes when you trust that what is meant to sustain you will arrive in the season you can actually carry it?

MICRO PRACTICE

ALIGN WHILE YOU WAIT

Waiting is not the same as doing nothing. There is passive waiting. And there is active waiting. Passive waiting watches the clock. Active waiting becomes the kind of person who can steward what is coming.

Choose one area of your life where you feel stuck waiting.

A relationship.
An opportunity.
A breakthrough.
A decision.
A next step.
A door that has not yet opened.

Write it down clearly, then ask yourself:

"What would the version of me who could sustain this well already be practicing?"

Do not focus only on what you want to receive.
Focus on who you are being invited to become.

Complete the following:

The thing I am waiting for is ____.

The version of me who can steward this well would be practicing ____.

One habit that would help me become more ready is ____.

One mindset I need to release while I wait is ____.

One action I can take this week to align with readiness is ____.

Now choose two or three actions.

Do them.
Not to force the outcome.
Not to manipulate timing.
Not to prove you deserve the blessing.
Do them because waiting can become a place of preparation.
Because readiness is built through repetition.
Because the person who receives the thing may need different rhythms than the person who first prayed for it.

Waiting is not inactivity.
It is preparation in motion.

CARRY THIS FORWARD

You are not behind. You are not late. You are not forgotten.

You may be impatient. You may be tired. You may be frustrated by the gap between what you can see and what you still believe is coming. That does not mean nothing is happening. It may mean something is being formed slowly enough to last.

Some blessings require more than desire. They require capacity. Discernment. Humility. Discipline. Healing. Room. And sometimes the waiting is where those things are developed.

So, do not rush past this season only because it feels uncomfortable. Do not mistake quiet for absence. Do not mistake delay for denial. Do not mistake stillness for failure. There may be work happening beneath the surface that your eyes are not yet trained to recognize. There may be preparation taking place in places you cannot measure. There may be alignment happening in conversations you are not part of, rooms you have not entered, and timing you would not have chosen.

Trust does not mean you stop wanting. It means you stop worshiping urgency. It means you continue becoming while you wait. It means you ask a better question than, *"When will it happen?"* You ask: *"Who am I becoming while I wait?"*

One day, you may look back and realize the waiting was not wasted. It was not empty. It was not punishment. It was the season that made you strong enough, steady enough, and whole enough to carry what was coming without being crushed by it.

Wait well. Prepare faithfully. And keep becoming.

YOUR BLESSING IS JUST BUFFERING

Waiting changes when you stop viewing it as empty space.

Because most of us imagine progress as something visible. A promotion. A milestone. A contract signed. A prayer answered. A door opening. A tangible sign that all our effort has been worth it. We like evidence. Metrics. Movement we can point to. Something we can hold up and say: "See? It's working."

But some of the most important work in life happens underground. Roots form before branches appear. Foundations are poured before buildings rise. Character develops long before opportunities arrive requiring it.

And yet, because we cannot see those things happening, we often assume nothing is happening at all. That assumption is expensive. It steals hope. Creates anxiety. Tempts us to abandon processes that are quietly working on our behalf.

The truth is that growth is rarely as visible as we want it to be. Sometimes your capacity is expanding before your opportunity arrives. Sometimes your wisdom is developing before your platform grows. Sometimes your healing is deepening before your circumstances change. Sometimes life is preparing you for something that would have crushed the version of you that existed six months ago.

The challenge is that preparation rarely looks impressive while it's happening. It often looks like ordinary days. Small choices. Consistent effort. Patience that nobody applauds. Faithfulness that nobody notices. Until one day, what seemed invisible becomes undeniable. And what felt delayed suddenly makes sense.

The next piece is an invitation to reconsider the seasons that feel stalled. To reconsider the moments that feel stuck. To reconsider the possibility that what feels like a pause may actually be progress. Because not everything that appears motionless is broken. Sometimes it's building. Sometimes it's loading. Sometimes it's preparing itself to meet you.

YOUR BLESSING IS JUST BUFFERING

You ever prayed and wondered "what's taking so long?"
Ever felt like you're sitting at your computer, staring at the screen, watching that little circle spin?
That cosmic loop of irritation.
You ever think to yourself: "Lord... I asked for an answer, not a loading screen."
You're looking at the wheel,
He's looking at the world.
You're checking the WIFI,
He's checking your willingness.
You're impatient with seconds.
He's preparing you for seasons.
Your blessing isn't broken.
It isn't denied.
It isn't even delayed.
It's just...
Buffering.

Buffering is not a stall.
It's a setup.
It's the pause where your spirit syncs with the version of you that can actually handle what you've been praying for.
Because God doesn't give miracles to the man who's still allergic to movement.
He gives blessings to the one who's finally ready to receive, not just request.
God is not a genie.
He's a gardener.
Your life is not Amazon Prime.
Blessings don't appear on your porch two days after the prayer.
They grow.
They stretch.
They strengthen.
And sometimes, you have to shed the version of you that prayed the prayer in order to become the version of that can receive the blessing.

Don't confuse buffering with abandonment.

Don't confuse silence with absence.
Don't confuse time with punishment.
Buffering is preparation.
A holy pause. A divine inhale.
A sacred recalibration of everything we think we want and everything God knows we need.
You keep asking, "God... where's my blessing?"
And God keeps saying, "Child... where's your readiness?"

You may think nothing is happening.
But God is programming the version of your life that matches your purpose.
You are being updated.
Upgraded.
Re-created.
Your storms didn't stop your blessing.
Your storms strengthened your bandwidth to carry it.
And one thing I've learned?
God isn't slow.
He's sequenced.
He's strategic.
He's sovereign.
Your blessing is not late.
Your blessing is just buffering.

NOTICING & INTEGRATION

FRUSTRATION & INTERPRETATION

When progress is invisible, frustration often starts filling in the blanks. We often assume nothing is happening because nothing is obvious. We often interpret silence as failure and stillness as proof that we are stuck.

- Where in your life do you currently feel like things are not moving?
- What assumptions are you making about that lack of visible progress?
- How are those assumptions affecting your mindset or behavior?
- On a scale of 1–10, how patient are you when you cannot see immediate results?
- What has helped you be even this patient so far?

HIDDEN WORK

Some growth happens beneath the surface before it becomes visible above ground. Capacity often develops quietly. There may be internal changes happening right now that have not yet become external results.

- What might be developing beneath the surface in this season of life?
- What internal changes have you experienced recently that others may not see?
- How might your capacity be increasing, even if your results are not visible yet?
- On a scale of 1–10, how much do you trust that progress can be happening even when it is invisible?
- What would be different if you were one point higher?

PATIENCE & PERSPECTIVE

A setback and a setup can feel almost identical while you are living through them. The difference is often revealed later. What feels slow may be strengthening you. What feels delayed may be protecting you.

- What would change if you believed this season was a setup, not a setback?
- How would you show up differently if you trusted the process more?
- What pressure would release if you stopped expecting fast results?
- On a scale of 1–10, how much are you able to remain steady while waiting for results to catch up with your effort?
- If that number moved one point higher, what would you stop checking, rushing, or trying to force?

WHAT'S ALREADY TRUE

You already have evidence that timing can become meaningful in hindsight. You have already lived through seasons where what looked slow, inconvenient, or unclear eventually made more sense. Even now, this season may be developing strengths you would not have built if everything had arrived immediately.

- When have you already experienced something taking longer than expected, but turning out better because of it?
- What changes when you believe progress may be happening, even when you cannot measure it yet?
- What strengths, disciplines, or capacities are you already developing in this season that you may not have built if everything had arrived immediately?

MICRO PRACTICE
NAME IT IN THE MOMENT

Impatience can become a spiral. One thought becomes ten. One delay becomes a conclusion. One unanswered question becomes evidence that nothing is working. This practice is designed to interrupt that spiral before it becomes the whole story.

Name something in your life that currently has you feeling impatient, frustrated, discouraged, or behind.

Write it down, then complete the following:

The thing that feels like it is not moving is ____.

The story I am tempted to tell about this delay is ____.

The pressure I feel because of this delay is ____.

Now pause. Take one deep, slow breath, then say:

"It's not broken. It's buffering."

Take another breath, then say it again:

"It's not broken. It's buffering."

Now ask yourself:

What if this is not proof that nothing is happening?

What if this is preparation I cannot fully see yet?

What if I can stay steady without needing constant confirmation?

Write one sentence that helps you reframe this moment. For example:

"I can remain faithful to the process even when I cannot yet see the result." "I do not have to rush what is still being prepared." "My responsibility is alignment, not obsession."

Keep that sentence somewhere visible.
Return to it when impatience gets loud.
Because what you name, you begin to reframe.
And what you reframe, you begin to carry differently.

CARRY THIS FORWARD

You do not need constant confirmation.

You do not need visible progress every day. You do not need proof at every step in order to keep moving with intention. What you need is steadiness. The ability to stay grounded when the results have not arrived yet. The ability to keep showing up when the evidence is still quiet. The ability to trust that progress is not only real when it is obvious.

So much of life is built in the unseen. Roots before fruit. Practice before performance. Formation before manifestation. Preparation before arrival. And yet, when we cannot see movement, we often assume we have been forgotten.

We start checking obsessively. Rushing unnecessarily. Comparing unfairly. Interpreting every delay as evidence that something has gone wrong. But your life is not always stuck simply because it is still. Your progress is not always paused because it is private. Your future is not always delayed because it has not yet introduced itself. Sometimes it is loading. Aligning. Recalibrating. Preparing itself to meet the version of you who will be ready to carry it.

So, the next time impatience rises, breathe before you conclude. Pause before you panic. Notice before you narrate. And remind yourself: It may not be broken. It may not be denied. It may not be over. It may simply be buffering.

I'M NEW TO THIS

One of the most surprising parts of growth is that arriving doesn't feel the way we imagined it would.

We spend years thinking the breakthrough will eliminate the struggle. That clarity will eliminate uncertainty. That healing will eliminate doubt. That maturity will eliminate mistakes. But then the opportunity arrives. The relationship arrives. The peace arrives. The new season arrives. And we discover something humbling. We're still learning. Still figuring things out. Still carrying questions. Still growing into the very things we once prayed for.

Because transformation is not an event. It's an adjustment. A learning curve. A series of small, imperfect repetitions that slowly become a new way of living.

And yet many of us struggle with that reality. We expect ourselves to perform mastery the moment growth appears. We assume that because we've learned something, we should automatically know how to embody it. Because we've healed something, we should never struggle with it again. Because we've prayed for something, we should know exactly how to carry it once it arrives. But becoming doesn't work that way.

The version of you that prayed for this season is not the same version of you learning how to live inside it. And that learning deserves grace. Patience. Compassion. Room to stumble without concluding you've failed. Because every new chapter comes with a learning curve. Every answered prayer introduces new responsibilities. Every level of growth requires new skills. And every transition asks us to become beginners again.

The next piece is an invitation to release the pressure of having it all figured out. To stop mistaking learning for failure. To stop confusing uncertainty with inadequacy. And to remember that growth has never required perfection. Only participation. Because the truth is... We are all still learning. And that's okay.

I'M NEW TO THIS

I'm not faking it until I make it, I'm just new to this.
But I'm really trying to be true to this.
And I need to say that with my chest.
Because I think sometimes people assume that faith arrives fully formed.
Like one day you just wake up, and everything makes sense.
Like fear disappears.
Like doubt packs its bags and leaves you alone with clarity.
I certainly did.
That hasn't been my experience.

My instinct has always been to rely on what I can reason through.
To trust what I can map out.
To make decisions based on logic.
On evidence.
On outcomes I can predict.
And if I'm honest, on fear.
Not loud fear.
Not the kind that announces itself.
But the quiet kind.
The kind that sounds like responsibility.
Like planning. Like "being smart."
The kind that keeps you safe but also keeps you small.

This whole journey of trusting God.
Of actually leaning into faith instead of just referencing it.
It's new.
It's uncomfortable.
Because faith doesn't always explain itself before asking you to move.
And I don't like moving without understanding.
I like clarity.
I like control.
I like knowing where the next step lands before I lift my foot.
But that's not how this works.
This feels more like being asked to walk with just enough light for the step I'm on.
And nothing more.
Some days I do it well.

Some days I wake up and I'm grounded. Centered.
Able to say, "Whatever You have for me, I trust it."
And I mean it.
And then there are other days.
Days where the questions come back.
Where the doubt gets louder.
Where I start trying to solve things that were never mine to control.
Days where I slip back into old patterns of thinking.
Where I start calculating instead of trusting.
Strategizing instead of surrendering.
Where faith feels less like confidence and more like effort.

But even in that, I'm still trying.
Trying to pause before I react.
Trying to listen longer than I speak.
Trying to choose alignment over instinct.
Trying to believe that what I don't understand is still working in my favor.
And that's the part I'm learning to respect.
That faith is not about perfection.
It's about participation.
It's about showing up again and again, even when you're unsure.
Even when you don't feel strong.
Even when the outcome isn't clear.
It's waking up and choosing trust on purpose.
Not because it's easy, but because it's necessary.
Necessary for the life you're being called into.

So, no, I don't have it all figured out.
I don't move without hesitation.
I don't always get it right.
But I'm moving.
I'm choosing.
I'm practicing.
I'm learning that that's what faith really is.
Not the absence of fear, but the decision to keep going anyway.
Not a destination you arrive at, but a rhythm you learn one step at a time.

So, if you see me walking this out, understand something...
I'm not pretending to be something I'm not.
I'm becoming something I've never been.

And I'm doing it in real time.
Learning as I go.
Trusting as I grow.
Falling forward.
Getting back up.
Trying again.
There is nothing fake about it.

I'm not sure I'll ever "make it," or what that even looks like.
I'm new to this.
But I'm really, truly, trying to be true to this.

NOTICING & INTEGRATION

TRUST VS. CONTROL

Many of us call it responsibility. Preparation. Being smart. Thinking ahead. But underneath those habits can sometimes be something deeper: the desire to avoid uncertainty. Trust asks us to move without certainty.

- Where in your life do you find yourself trying to control outcomes instead of trusting the process?
- What fears tend to disguise themselves as "being responsible" or "thinking logically"?
- What would it look like to loosen your grip, even slightly, on needing certainty before you move?
- On a scale of 1–10, how willing are you to move forward without having everything figured out?
- What would you do tomorrow If you were one ooint higher?

FAITH IN REAL TIME

Faith often sounds beautiful in theory, but feels much messier in practice. Faith in real time looks less like certainty and more like participation.

- What parts of your journey currently feel unfamiliar, uncomfortable, or unresolved?
- When have you continued moving despite feeling uncertain?
- What does "trying to be true to this" look like in your life right now?
- On a scale of 1–10, how much do you trust yourself to keep growing even when the process feels uncomfortable?
- What makes it that number and not lower?

BECOMING

We often treat growth like a destination. Something we arrive at. Something we eventually master. But becoming is rarely a finish line. What old ways of thinking are hardest for you to release?

- Where do you notice yourself growing, even if the growth feels slow?
- What would change if you stopped expecting yourself to arrive and focused instead on continuing to practice?
- On a scale of 1–10, how connected do you currently feel to the version of yourself you are becoming?
- If that number moved one point higher, what would you stop overthinking and what would become easier to trust?

WHAT'S ALREADY TRUE

Growth is often easier to recognize looking backward than looking forward. You may already be practicing new ways of thinking, responding, trusting, or showing up. Even if you have not given yourself credit for them yet.

- What are you already doing that suggests you may be growing more than you realize?
- When have you recently responded to a challenge differently than an earlier version of yourself would have?
- What changes when you trust that you do not need to have everything figured out in order to keep moving forward?

MICRO PRACTICE
FAITH IN PROCESS

There is a difference between being lost and being new. When we are new to something, uncertainty is not evidence of failure. It is evidence of learning. This practice is designed to help you honor the process instead of judging yourself for being in it.

Complete the following:

WHAT'S NEW

What feels new, unfamiliar, or uncomfortable for me right now is ____.

What makes this challenging is ____.

What I wish I already knew is ____.

MY DEFAULT RESPONSE

When I feel uncertain, my instinct is to ____.

When I do this, it helps me by ____.

But it sometimes limits me by ____.

THE PERSON I'M BECOMING

The version of me I am becoming practices ____.

When uncertainty shows up, they remind themselves ____.

One way I can practice becoming that person this week is ____.

PERMISSION

Write the following exactly:

"I am allowed to be learning."

"Progress does not require perfection."

"Trying sincerely is still movement."

Now, read each statement aloud. Slowly.

Notice which one feels easiest to believe.
Notice which one feels hardest.
Spend a few moments with the one you most need to hear.

CARRY THIS FORWARD

You do not have to look polished to be progressing.

You do not have to feel certain to be faithful. You do not have to stop being human in order to become transformed. Because becoming is messy. It is uneven. It is honest. Some days trust feels natural. Some days it feels like effort. Some days you move confidently. Some days you take the next step while quietly wondering if you are doing any of this correctly.

Both count. Read that again. Both count.

Growth is not measured by how confidently you speak. Faith is not measured by how few questions you have. Transformation is not measured by how perfectly you perform. They are measured by something much simpler: *Do you keep showing up? Do you keep choosing? Do you keep returning? Do you keep practicing?*

Because the people you admire most were once beginners too. The people who are grounded once felt uncertain. The people who are confident once felt new. They did not become who they are by waiting until they felt ready. They became who they are by participating before they felt prepared.

So, release the pressure to perform certainty. Release the fantasy that everyone else has figured it out. Release the lie that struggle means you are failing.

You are not behind. You are not broken. You are not disqualified because you are still learning. You are becoming. And becoming has always been a process. Not a performance.

So, keep going. Not because you have mastered it. Because you are willing to learn it.

WILL YOU TRANSITION?

There comes a moment in every transformation journey when preparation has done all it can do.

Not because preparation isn't valuable. Because eventually preparation must become participation. You can spend years gathering insight. Years collecting wisdom. Years understanding your patterns. Years identifying what needs to change. Years waiting for the perfect moment. The perfect plan. The perfect feeling. The perfect version of yourself. And still remain standing exactly where you started. Not because you lack potential. Because potential has a limitation. Potential only matters when it moves. At some point, every lesson becomes an invitation. Every realization becomes a responsibility. Every prayer becomes a decision.

Because awareness alone does not change a life. Alignment alone does not change a life. Intention alone does not change a life. Movement changes a life. Action changes a life. Participation changes a life. And perhaps that is why transition is so difficult. Not because we don't know what to do. Most of us know far more than we practice. Not because we lack clarity. Many of us have been receiving clarity for years. The challenge is that transition asks us to leave the safety of preparation and enter the uncertainty of becoming. It asks us to stop studying the map and begin walking the road. To stop rehearsing the conversation and begin speaking. To stop imagining the future and begin participating in it. And that can feel terrifying.

Because movement creates risk. Movement creates vulnerability. Movement creates the possibility of failure. But it also creates the possibility of transformation. The possibility of becoming the person you've spent this entire journey preparing to be.

The truth is that there are seasons for searching. Seasons for healing. Seasons for waiting. Seasons for learning. And then there are seasons for moving. In the seasons, the question is no longer: *"What do you know?"* The question is no longer: *"What do you believe?"* The question is no longer: *"What are you waiting for?"* The question is much simpler. And much harder. The question is: *Will You Transition?*

WILL YOU TRANSITION?

It's easy to pray for harvest, but harder to till the soil.
Everybody wants abundance but not everybody wants the blisters that come with blessing.
Pastor Davis said, "you can't just align, you have to transition."
And I felt that.
Because alignment gets you ready, but transition gets you there.
See, when two things align, it means they're parallel.
But transition...Transition is movement.
It's when the idea stops being inspirational and becomes operational.
It's when the assignment stops visiting your thoughts and starts living in your body.
It's when your purpose stops being an idea and starts breathing in your chest.

You cannot cry about empty fields when your hands never learned the language of planting.
You cannot starve in a season of potential and blame God for what discipline refused to build.
Because there is a difference between waiting on the Lord and wasting time.
One is faithful. The other is fear with better branding.

Stalled at orientation, still expecting elevation.
Fruit without formation, harvest, no preparation.
Prayer with no participation stalls manifestation.
Multiplication needs discipline, and dedication.
God's math isn't random, it's precise calibration.
Every step accounted in divine administration.
You don't skip the process and arrive at transformation.
Favor finds the faithful through consistent cultivation.

God does not miscalculate.
What you plant will find you again.
Not always when you want it.
Not always how you expect it.
But always on time.
That's not coincidence.
That's covenant.

See, alignment is divine.
But transition is divine and disciplined.
It's God whispering, "You ready," and you whispering back, "Let's go."
It's shedding the skin that once kept you safe because now it's too small for the spirit you're in.
It's not enough to recognize the assignment, you have to walk it.
You can't stay a caterpillar praying for wings and call that faith.
At some point you have to break your own cocoon.
Metamorphosis demands you abandon what was comfortable.
Every elevation asks something of you.
There is no version of growth that does not require release.
No calling that arrives without first confronting the parts of you still negotiating with fear.

And fear will speak.
Loudly. Logically. Convincingly.
It will disguise itself as caution.
As wisdom. As responsibility.
But purpose does not unfold through constant negotiation with comfort.
It requires movement.
Pressure. Positioning.
The willingness to outgrow what once made you feel protected.
Because sometimes the thing that feels unfamiliar is not wrong.
It's inevitable.
And what you call disruption might actually be the first honest sign that your life is beginning to align with what it was always meant to become.

And let me be clear: transition does not remove fear, it repositions it.
Fear doesn't disappear, it just loses authority.
Because faith is not the absence of fear.
Faith is the refusal to let fear make decisions about your destiny.
You will feel it.
You will question it.
You will stand at the edge of everything you prayed for and still wonder if you're ready.
That's normal.
That's human.
That's the moment where calling asks for commitment.
Not perfection. Commitment.

Because God is not waiting for you to be flawless.
He is waiting for you to be faithful.
To keep moving when the outcome is unclear.
To keep planting when the soil feels silent.
To keep showing up when the results haven't introduced themselves yet.

So, I ask you: will you transition?
Will you move once alignment has confirmed the direction, but not the coordinates?
Will you step when the door is open, but the room is unfamiliar?
Will you become what you've been praying about?
Because belief is not enough.
Alignment is not enough.
Even prayer is not enough.
At some point you have to move from "Amen" to "I'm in."
Not just spiritually.
Physically.
Practically.
Consistently.
Because harvest does not respond to your plans.
It responds to your obedience.
And obedience is action.

NOTICING & INTEGRATION

AWARENESS VS. ACTION

Insight is valuable. Awareness matters. Understanding yourself can be transformational. But awareness alone does not change your life. At some point, every realization asks a follow-up question: *Now what?*

- What do you already know you need to do, but have not yet done?
- Where in your life have you been aligned for a while, but not moving?
- What have you been calling preparation that might be avoidance?
- On a scale of 1–10, how consistently are your actions aligned with what you already know to be true?
- What would different if that number were one point higher?

FEAR & RESISTANCE

Most transitions are not blocked by information. They are blocked by fear. Fear of failure. Fear of judgment. Fear of success. Fear of becoming responsible for the life you say you want.

- What fears emerge when you think about taking action?
- What are you protecting yourself from by staying where you are?
- What is the cost of remaining exactly where you are for another year?
- On a scale of 1–10, how willing are you to experience temporary discomfort in service of long-term growth?
- If that number moved one point higher, what fear would have less influence over your decisions?

COMMITMENT

The difference between wishing and becoming is often commitment. Commitment is what happens when a decision survives inconvenience. Transition is not a feeling. It is a series of repeated choices.

- What would it look like to fully commit? Not just mentally, but behaviorally?
- What action have you been postponing that would meaningfully move your life forward?
- What version of yourself are you delaying by refusing to act?
- On a scale of 1–10, how committed are you to following through, even when it becomes uncomfortable?
- If that number moved one point higher, what excuse would no longer be allowed to make decisions for you?

WHAT'S ALREADY TRUE

You are not starting from zero. You have already survived difficult transitions. You have already taken steps you once believed you were incapable of taking. There is probably more evidence of courage in your story than your fear wants you to remember.

- What are you already doing that suggests you are closer to your goals than you think?
- When have you already taken action before you felt ready? What did that experience teach you about yourself?
- What changes when you stop asking whether you are ready and start asking whether you are willing?

MICRO PRACTICE
THE TRANSITION PLAN

A transition is not an intention. It is movement. This exercise is designed to help you move from reflection into participation.
Choose one area of your life where you know it is time to move.

Not someday. Not eventually. Now.

Complete the following:

"I am transitioning from ____ to ____."

Be specific.
The more honest you are, the more useful this becomes.

Then, complete the following:

THE REALITY

The thing I know is no longer serving me is ____.

The reason I have stayed here longer than I needed to is ____.

The cost of staying is ____.

THE DECISION

The future I want to move toward is ____.

The person I am becoming is someone who ____.

The decision I am making today is ____.

THE ACTION

One action I will take today is ____.

One action I will take this week is ____.

One action I will practice consistently is ____.

THE COMMITMENT

"Even if I do not feel ready, I am willing to ____."

Read it aloud.
Then read it again.

Because transitions do not begin when fear disappears.
They begin when willingness becomes stronger than fear.

CARRY THIS FORWARD

You do not need more clarity.

You do not need another sign. You do not need one more book, one more podcast, one more conversation, or one more month to think about it. At some point, preparation becomes procrastination wearing a respectable outfit.

You already know more than enough to begin. Not enough to control the outcome. Enough to take the next step. And that is all transitions have ever required. Not certainty. Participation.

The future you keep imagining is not waiting for perfect conditions. It is waiting for your involvement. Waiting for your decision. Waiting for your willingness to move before every fear has been resolved.

Because courage is not the absence of fear. It is movement in its presence. So let this be the moment. Not the moment you prepare. Not the moment you plan. Not the moment you promise yourself that one day you will finally begin.

Let this be the moment you decide. The moment you stop standing at the threshold. The moment you stop asking whether the door is open. The moment you walk through it.

Your future is not waiting on your potential. It is waiting on your participation. The question has never been whether transition is possible.

The question is: *Will you?* And if your answer is yes, take the step. Today.

GOD IS GOOD ALL THE TIME

The funny thing about transition is that you rarely understand it while it's happening.

While you're in it, it feels like uncertainty. Like risk. Like letting go before you're ready. Like trusting without enough evidence. Like stepping away from what was familiar without fully knowing what comes next. Transition feels messy up close. Disorienting. Incomplete. Which is why most of life's deepest lessons only become visible when we look back. Because hindsight has a way of revealing what fear tried to hide. The connection between events that once seemed random. The preparation hidden inside disappointment. The protection hidden inside delay. The opportunities concealed within endings. The grace woven through moments that felt ordinary at the time.

And perhaps that is one of the greatest gifts of growth. Not that it changes the past. But that it changes how we understand it. The same experience that once felt like rejection begins to look like redirection. The same season that once felt like punishment begins to look like preparation. The same unanswered prayer begins to look like protection. Not because the hardship wasn't real. Not because the pain wasn't painful. But because perspective allows us to see more than the moment itself. It allows us to see the thread. The pattern. The fingerprints. The quiet evidence that something larger may have been at work all along.

If you've made it this far in the journey, perhaps you've already begun noticing those moments. Moments that make you pause and wonder: *What if I wasn't nearly as alone as I thought? What if more was happening than I could see? What if grace had been showing up long before I learned how to recognize it?*

Because eventually every transition creates an opportunity. An opportunity to look backward. To connect the dots. To reconsider the story. And to recognize that what once felt random may have been meaningful all along.

The next piece is not about certainty. It's about recognition. The kind that arrives when you finally look back and see what was there the entire time.

GOD IS GOOD ALL THE TIME

God is good all the time.
Even when I wasn't looking.
Especially when I wasn't looking.
I spent the first few decades of my life arguing with the sky.
Rolling my eyes at miracles.
Mistaking intellect for immunity.
Thinking disbelief made me bulletproof.
There were seasons I didn't just doubt, I debated.
Built arguments like scaffolding.
Invited people to climb them with me.
Pointed at the heavens and said, "See? Nothing there."
And still.
Every turn I took.
Every door I slammed.
Every wilderness detour I called freedom.
God was there.
Quiet. Unoffended. Unrushed.
Blessing me anyway.

Misguided ambition, dressed up as precision.
I called it independence, God called it revision.
Debated His existence with academic derision.
Still, He authored outcomes beyond my limited vision.
Provision in the drought, mercy in collision.
Favor in the fallout, blessing in omission.
Every "random" rescue was sacred composition.
I was lost in translation, He was steady in position.

Looking back, I see it now.
The jobs that arrived right when the landlord was ready to evict me.
The mentors who showed up disguised as coincidence.
The narrow misses that should have been headlines.
The pain that didn't kill me but taught me language.
I thought I was wandering.
Turns out I was walking a path I just didn't have the vocabulary for yet.
God never forced Himself into my sentence.
That's real love.
That's trust.

That's sovereignty without ego.
Because love that isn't chosen is just control wearing a choir robe.
God gave me room.
Room to wrestle. Room to run.
Room to build a whole identity out of being wrong about Him.
Thirty plus years in the wilderness and not once did He revoke provision.
Not once did He snatch the calling back.
Not once did He say, "you took too long."

Misread the map, didn't understand the assignment.
He let me roam free, never canceled the consignment.
I questioned the source, tried to reframe the requirement.
Internal refinement through seasons of confinement.
I didn't recognize Him, somehow still walked in compliance.
I named it my work, He named it His environment.
Service as evidence, calling in silence.
He stayed present, unmoved by my defiance.
That's grace without pressure, that's love without violence.

I see now that even when I didn't say His name I was doing His work.
Serving people. Advocating for dignity.
Standing between harm and hope.
Speaking truth with a trembling voice.
I didn't recognize the calling but the calling recognized me.
God is good all the time.
Even when we misname the source of our strength.
Even when we call grace "luck."
Even when we call mercy "timing."
Even when we call purpose "accident."

I don't walk perfectly now, let's be clear about that.
I still miss steps.
Still get distracted.
Still need reminders to slow down longer.
To listen more and speak less.
But I walk aligned.
And alignment feels different than perfection.
It feels lighter.
Truer.

Like my soul finally exhaled after holding its breath for decades.
Now I know.
Everything I have is borrowed.
Every gift.
Every insight.
Every platform.
Every door.
I am not the source.
I am a conduit.
A vessel.
A messenger.
One piece of a divine mosaic that only makes sense when it reflects more than itself.

That's the responsibility.
That's the honor.
To use what I've been given for more than applause.
To let blessing become service.
To let testimony become invitation.
God has been walking with you.
Patient.
Faithful.
Leaving breadcrumbs of grace in places you thought were dead ends.
You don't have to be perfect to turn around.
You don't have to have the language yet.
You don't even have to be sure, just willing.
God is good all the time.
And all the time God is good.

NOTICING & INTEGRATION

PRESENCE & PERSPECTIVE

Sometimes grace is easiest to recognize in hindsight. Perspective does not erase what was hard, but it can help us recognize what sustained us through it.

- Looking back on your life, where do you now recognize grace that you previously dismissed as coincidence?
- What moments, relationships, opportunities, or near-misses feel different when viewed through the lens of purpose instead of luck?
- On a scale of 1–10, how open are you to recognizing support, provision, or guidance in parts of your story you once interpreted differently?
- What experiences have helped that openness become as strong as it already is?

WRESTLING & DOUBT

Faith does not always arrive quietly. Sometimes it comes through questions. Doubt does not always mean absence of faith. Sometimes doubt is doorway through which a more honest faith begins to form.

- In what ways have you been "arguing with the sky" in your own life?
- What would it mean to admit that uncertainty and openness can exist at the same time?
- On a scale of 1–10, how willing are you to remain open even when you do not have complete certainty?
- What helps you stay open without pretending you have every answer?

CALLING & ALIGNMENT

Purpose often leaves a trail before we have language for it. We may find ourselves drawn toward certain people, certain work, certain causes, or certain forms of service long before we understand why.

- What parts of your story make more sense when viewed through the lens of purpose rather than randomness?
- What gifts, strengths, or opportunities feel bigger than something you created entirely on your own?
- On a scale of 1–10, how aligned do you feel between what you believe, what you value, and how you are living?
- If that number moved one point higher, what would you release, trust, or practice differently this week?

WHAT'S ALREADY TRUE

Your story may already contain more evidence of grace than you first noticed. Support may have arrived before you called it support. Provision may have appeared before you had language for provision. Purpose may have been moving through your life before you knew how to name it.

- What experiences in your life already suggest you have been guided, supported, protected, or sustained more than you realized at the time?
- What strengths, gifts, relationships, or opportunities already point to purpose moving through your story?
- What changes when you believe you do not have to understand every step in order to move forward with intention?

MICRO PRACTICE
TRACE THE EVIDENCE

Sometimes faith begins with looking again. Not forcing certainty. Not rewriting history to make every painful moment feel easy. Simply looking again with enough openness to ask: Was I more accompanied than I realized?

Think of a season in your life when you felt lost, disconnected, uncertain, spiritually distant, or convinced you were on your own.

Write that season at the top of the page, then complete this sentence:

"There was a season when I believed ____."

Sit with that sentence.
Let it tell the truth about how that season felt.

Next, identify moments from that season that you can see differently now.

Maybe a person showed up.
A door opened.
A door closed.
A bill got paid.
A warning came just in time.
A relationship shifted.
A rejection redirected you.
A strength emerged that you did not know you had.

For each moment, complete the following:

"At the time, I called this ____."

"Now I wonder if it may have been ____."

Then, complete this final sentence:

"What I thought was abandonment may have actually been ____."

Do not force the answer.
Let it breathe.
This practice is not about pretending every season was easy.
It is about expanding your interpretation.
It is about making room for the possibility that grace was present even before you knew what to call it.

CARRY THIS FORWARD

Sometimes faith does not begin with revelation.

Sometimes it begins with recognition. With looking back and realizing you were never nearly as alone as you thought. That provision kept showing up. That mercy kept interrupting outcomes. That grace kept writing in margins you never noticed. Not always loudly. Not always dramatically.

Not always in ways you understood at the time. But still there. Still present. Still patient. Still working.

Maybe you called it luck. Maybe you called it timing. Maybe you called it coincidence. Maybe you called it survival. Maybe you gave yourself full credit because that was the only explanation you had. And perhaps some of that credit was deserved.

You did survive. You did keep going. You did make choices that mattered.

But maybe your strength was not the absence of grace. Maybe your resilience was one of its expressions. You do not need airtight theology to begin noticing. You do not need perfect certainty to practice gratitude. You do not need to understand every step to move forward with intention. You only need enough humility to look again. To reconsider the story. To wonder whether something larger may have been present, even when your language was limited.

So, pause.

Look back gently. Look forward honestly. And remember: What you once called coincidence may have always been care. What you once called survival may have also been sustaining grace. And what you once believed you did alone may have been a journey God was walking with you the entire time.

BEFORE YOU GO

Perhaps the greatest gift of perspective is not that it changes the past.

It's that it changes the present. Because once you begin recognizing grace in hindsight, something shifts. You stop demanding certainty before taking the next step. You stop treating every unanswered question like a crisis. You stop assuming that every delay means something has gone wrong. Not because life suddenly becomes easier. Because you've seen enough evidence to trust differently.

You've seen how seemingly unrelated moments connected. How closed doors redirected you. How painful seasons refined you. How opportunities appeared at precisely the right time. How strength emerged from places you never would have chosen. And once you've seen that pattern enough times, faith begins to mature.

It becomes less about prediction and more about participation. Less about guarantees and more about trust. Less about needing to know exactly what's next and more about knowing who walks beside you when you get there. That doesn't mean every question has been answered. It doesn't mean every wound has fully healed. It doesn't mean every chapter has been resolved. It simply means you've learned something essential: You can keep moving before the entire story makes sense.

Because life is not a puzzle to solve. It is a journey to live. And if you've made it this far, leaning into the opportunity, you've already done something remarkable. You've searched. You've reflected. You've released. You've trusted. You've waited. You've learned. You've remembered. Most importantly, you've practiced telling yourself the truth. The truth about who you are. The truth about what matters. The truth about what you're no longer willing to carry. The truth about what you're becoming.

And now, there is only one thing left to do. Take what you've discovered and bring it with you. Beyond these pages. Beyond these poems. Beyond this moment. Because books can inspire. Questions can illuminate. Poetry can awaken. But transformation happens in the living.

If you've made it here, don't rush past this moment. Not because this is the end. Because it isn't. A book can end. A journey cannot.

What you've just walked through was never intended to be a collection of poems alone. It was an invitation. An invitation to pause. To notice. To remember. To question. To release. To trust. To become.

Some of these pages may have felt familiar. Some may have felt uncomfortable. Some may have given language to things you had been carrying for years without knowing how to name them. And if you allowed yourself to engage honestly, you probably recognized something along the way: This was never just my story. It was yours too.

Maybe you saw yourself in the waiting. Maybe you saw yourself in the grief. Maybe you saw yourself in the striving. Maybe you saw yourself in the silence. Maybe you saw yourself in the moment when you realized you were exhausted from carrying things that no longer belonged to you. Maybe you saw yourself in the slow and sacred work of becoming.

Whatever brought you here, I hope you leave knowing this: You are not broken. You are not behind. You are not disqualified. You are not too late. And you are certainly not alone.

Because beneath every poem was a simple truth. One that kept resurfacing in different forms, wearing different clothes, speaking different languages. *You were never abandoned.* Not in the confusion. Not in the delay. Not in the disappointment. Not in the silence. Not even in the moments when you felt furthest from yourself.

God was there.

Not always loudly. Not always in ways you recognized. Not always in ways that made immediate sense. But present. Patient. Faithful. Walking beside you through every chapter.

And maybe now you can see what you couldn't see before. Maybe what felt like a detour was direction. Maybe what felt like loss was protection. Maybe what felt like waiting was preparation. Maybe what felt like breaking was transformation. Maybe what felt like the end was actually an invitation to begin again.

This collection was never about perfection. It was about alignment. About learning to hear your own voice. About learning to trust God's. About releasing what no longer belongs. About receiving what does. About remembering that healing is not a destination.

It is a practice. Faith is not a destination. It is a practice. Love is not a destination. It is a practice. Becoming is not a destination. It is a practice. And practices require returning.

So, when life gets loud again, return. When fear gets louder than faith, return. When old stories try to reclaim authority, return. When you forget who you are, return. Return to this book. Return to what is true. Return to what matters. Return to the version of yourself that knows how to breathe, trust, love, release, and begin again. And above all else, remember this: *You do not have to walk perfectly. You only have to keep walking.*

One step. One prayer. One choice. One act of courage at a time. The title of this book was never a statement. It was always a question. *Will You Transition?*

Only you can answer that. But if these pages have taught you anything, I hope it is this: *You already have everything you need to begin.*

So, take the step. Trust the process. Honor the journey. And wherever the road leads next...walk it.

FINAL MICRO PRACTICE
THE COVENANT

You have traveled a long way to arrive here. You have examined old stories. You have listened to forgotten parts of yourself. You have released what no longer belongs. You have practiced new ways of thinking, new ways of trusting, and new ways of becoming. And now, you stand where every transformation ultimately leads. At an inflection point.

Because insight alone does not change a life. Awareness alone does not change a life. Even inspiration, by itself, does not change a life. A life changes when a person decides. This is your invitation to decide. Not who you have been. Not who others expected you to be. But who you are choosing to become.

Complete each of the following:

Take your time.
Write honestly. Write boldly.
Write as if your future self will someday read these words and remember this moment.

WHAT I AM LEAVING
Some things cannot come with you.

I am no longer available for ______.

I release the belief that ______.

The story I am retiring is ______.

What I have outgrown is ______.

WHAT I AM CHOOSING
Every "yes" creates a future. What future are you choosing?

I choose a life characterized by ______.

The values guiding this next chapter are ______.

I want more ______ in my life.

I want less ______ in my life.

The life I am building looks like ______.

WHAT I TRUST

There will be seasons when clarity feels limited. There will be moments when fear returns. There will be days when the path ahead feels uncertain. When those moments come, what truth will anchor you?

Even when I cannot see clearly, I will trust ______.

When uncertainty rises, I will remind myself that ______.

What I know to be true about myself is ______.

What I know to be true about God is ______.

WHAT I PRACTICE

Transformation is not sustained by motivation but by repetition.

When fear returns, I will return to ______.

The practices that keep me aligned are ______.

Instead of reacting from old patterns, I will choose to ______.

The person I want to become is strengthened each time I ______.

WHO I AM BECOMING

This journey has never been about perfection. It has always been about becoming.

I am becoming someone who ______.

The version of me I am growing into is someone who ______.

I want to be remembered as someone who ______.

The legacy I hope to leave is ______.

MY COMMITMENT

At some point, reflection becomes commitment. This is that moment.

Because of what I now know, I am choosing ______.

The next courageous step in my life is ______.

I will take that step by ______.

Now pause.
Read everything you have written.
Not quickly.
Not critically.
Read it as a witness to your own becoming.

Then, write the following exactly as it appears:

I will transition.

I will trust what I have learned.

I will honor who I am becoming.

I will keep moving, even when I cannot yet see the whole path.

I will not abandon myself.

I will not abandon my purpose.

I will become everything I was created to be.

LET'S CONTINUE THE CONVERSATION

If *Will You Transition?* resonated with you, imagine what this work can do inside your organization, school, conference, church, or community.

JONATHAN OFFERS TRANSFORMATIVE EXPERIENCES FOR TEAMS AND AUDIENCES THROUGH:

keynote speaking
conference plenaries
leadership development
therapeutic workshops
storytelling performances
custom curriculum design
strategic facilitation

INTERESTED IN:

bulk book orders?
workshop experiences?
keynote speaking?
leadership retreats?

SCAN BELOW:

VISIT:

www.karimasolutions.com

OR EMAIL:

info@karimasolutions.com

Healing should not be a luxury.
And yet for far too many individuals, couples, and families, access to quality mental health care remains financially out of reach.
That reality matters deeply to me.

As a therapist, I have seen firsthand what happens when people are ready for healing but cannot access support. I believe that access to transformative care should not be reserved only for those with financial privilege.

That is why

50% OF NET PROFITS FROM EVERY SALE OF

Will You Transition?

ARE DIRECTED TO THE KARIMA THERAPY ACCESS FUND.

The KARIMA Therapy Access Fund exists to help subsidize therapy services for individuals, couples, and families who would otherwise be unable to afford care.
Because healing multiplies. Stories matter.
And transformed lives create transformed communities.

WANT TO HELP EXPAND ACCESS EVEN FURTHER?
Scan the QR code below to make a direct contribution.

or visit:
www.karimasolutions.com/donate

THANK YOU FOR HELPING MAKE HEALING MORE ACCESSIBLE!

www.ingramcontent.com/pod-product-compliance
Lightning Source LLC
LaVergne TN
LVHW090517110826
845146LV00003B/890

* 9 7 9 8 9 5 0 8 9 4 0 0 8 *